mini New York

The Essential **Visitors'** Guide

New York mini Explorer – 1st Edition
ISBN 13 – 978-976-8182-94-4
ISBN 10 – 976-8182-94-6

Copyright © Explorer Group Ltd 2007
All rights reserved.

All maps © Explorer Group Ltd 2007

Front cover photograph – Times Square – Pamela Grist

Printed and bound by
Emirates Printing Press, Dubai, UAE

Explorer Publishing & Distribution
PO Box 34275, Zomorrodah Building,
Za'abeel Rd, Dubai , United Arab Emirates
Phone (+971 4) 335 3520   **Fax** (+971 4) 335 3529
Email Info@explorerpublishing.com
Web www.explorerpublishing.com

There's a lot to see and do in New York – you don't want to waste your energy lugging round a huge guidebook, which is where this teeny tiny little guide comes in handy. It's small enough to slide right into your pocket, yet it packs an informative punch. It's got info on visa requirements (p.14) and travel information (p.16), as well as restaurant and bar reviews (p.190), the lowdown on sports and spas (p.144) and everything you need to know about Manhattan's sizzling shopping scene (p.160). All information has been written by long-time residents of New York, so that you can benefit from the secrets only locals know.

The Explorer Team

Contents

Essentials

New York, New York

From the sky-high views and the great bars to the gothic architecture and the tangible energy, there's plenty to love about New York.

Does New York need introducing? Not really – you've seen it in countless movies and TV shows, splashed across magazine spreads and featured in works of art. In fact you could say that even if you've never been there, you'll feel like you have because everything is just so familiar.

It's the largest city in America, and one of the largest in the world, with a population of over eight million. Thanks to some much-needed reforms in the late 80s and early 90s, it's also the safest city in the US.

Although it is most famous for its many skyscrapers, this city of islands also has around 578 miles of waterfront, including 14 miles of public beach.

New York is the undisputed centre of American media, with two national newspapers, all four major American television networks, a dozen cable networks, and several film studios based in town. Hundreds of museums, art galleries and performance venues flourish.

An exceptionally diverse population has its benefits – you can get just about anything you need from anywhere in the world, at any time in New York. Certain areas of the city house concentrated populations of certain nationalities – areas like Chinatown, Little Italy and Spanish Harlem need no further explanation, but you will stumble upon other areas, such as East 32nd street in Midtown which is fast becoming New York's very own 'Koreatown'. A stroll through any of these areas will provide shopping and eating experiences that are as authentic as they are colourful.

New York is big and bold, and it can be overwhelming, particularly if you only have a few days. This chapter is meant to help you get your bearings and begin exploring from the moment you land at JFK. The checklist on p.6 is a perfect place to get started, outlining 12 must-do attractions or activities. The 'Best of New York' section on p.10 provides suggested itineraries based on whether you have a huge budget, are travelling with children, you're trying to cover the city on the cheap, or you are after the lowdown on the city's fascinating cultural scene.

New York Checklist

Central Park
Escape the New York buzz for a while and explore the vast green areas of Central Park (p.104). Join the joggers, hire a bike, or take a romantic horse-drawn carriage ride. Winter ice skating and summer concerts make this the ultimate year-round attraction.

Times Square
This iconic, neon-lit, pulsating heart of the city (p.89) overwhelms the senses from every angle. It's busy and noisy, but it's a great place to visit as soon as you arrive, or whenever you need reminding you're in the city that never sleeps.

Brooklyn Bridge
Take a walk from Manhattan to Brooklyn across this bridge (p.125) to enjoy amazing views of the city and the East River. The bridge itself is a beauty, with gothic towers and swirls of cables. Cross over at sunset for the most memorable views of Manhattan.

Ground Zero & St Paul's Chapel

Pay tribute to the victims and celebrate the tenacity of the survivors at the site of the 9/11 attacks (p.51), then visit nearby St Paul's Chapel (p.68), which escaped unscathed and was the makeshift resting place for hundreds of rescue workers.

New York Checklist

Shopping on Fifth Avenue

Make like Audrey Hepburn and hang out in Tiffany's (p.186), or just march down the sidewalk with a bundle of designer shopping bags hanging off your arm. If your budget doesn't stretch to Chanel, there's plenty of mid-range stores too (p.180).

Statue of Liberty

Lady Liberty (p.136) has welcomed people to New York since 1886 and was a particularly poignant symbol of freedom for early immigrants arriving at nearby Ellis Island (p.127). Get great views of this icon from the Staten Island Ferry.

Choose the Right Views

The Empire State Building (p.88) has sky-high views over the city and an inspiring art-deco interior. It also has long queues – head for the lesser-known 'Top of the Rock' at the Rockefeller Center (p.86) for similar views without the queues!

Eat at a Deli

New York has some great delis, where delicious food is freshly prepared with speed and a smile. Pop into Katz's (p.217) – it's one of the city's oldest delis, and also the most famous thanks to Meg Ryan's classic faking scene in When Harry Met Sally.

Helicopter Tour

Splurge on a whirlwind ride over the city for some awesome views (p.141). You have to book in advance and arrive early, but it's worth it when you find yourself sailing over the statue of Liberty with your stomach still somewhere at ground level.

Arty Museums

New York has some of the best galleries and museums in the world – a mooch around the spiral-shaped Guggenheim (p.107), the Metropolitan Museum of Art (p.108), or the Museum of Modern Art (p.88), provides candy for the eyes and soul.

Sip a Cosmo in the MPD

The Meatpacking District (p.52) has lost its burly butchers in dirty aprons and gained a hip generation with Jimmy Choos and a serious cocktail habit – join them at Gin Lane (p.200) or Tenjune (p.202), or any other of the hotspots in the area.

Score a Bargain

Head for department stores like Century 21 (p.174) and Loehmann's (p.75) where you can get unbelievable bargains on some truly beautiful designer threads – just make sure you have enough time to rummage through the random rails!

Best of New York

For Big Spenders...

If you've got money to burn, New York is the ideal place to start the fire. Check into the Hotel on Rivington (p.38) for a luxurious suite and breathtaking views of the city through your panoramic floor-to-ceiling windows. Head to Fifth Avenue (p.166) for some top-end designer shopping, before resting your Manolo-heeled feet for a posh afternoon tea at the Rotunda inside the Pierre Hotel (p.233). Spend the afternoon being pampered from head to toe and sipping champagne at the lavish Cornelia Day Resort (p.156), before ending the day at one of the city's top restaurants – try Jean Georges (p.235), Nobu (p.243) or Balthazar (p.242).

For Families...

Rent some bicycles and race each other round Central Park (p.204), or if it's winter, get your skates on and practise your figures of eight on the Wollman Rink (p.149). Head to Bubby's Pie Company (p.240) for some American comfort food – even fussy little eaters will love the mac and cheese – before having a wander around the kid-friendly Museum of the City of New York (p.108), which has exhibits on virtually every aspect of life in the city. Visit FAO Schwarz (p.186), where you can dance on the giant piano featured in the movie Big, build your own Hot Wheels car, or design a luxurious doll's house. Catch a performance by the Paper Bag Players (www.thepaperbagplayers.com), a group of kooky adults performing original theatre for children aged 4 to 9.

For Budget Travellers...

Book a bunkbed at the trendy Gershwin Hotel (p.37) for around $40 a night – it doubles as an art gallery and is in the fascinating Chelsea neighbourhood. Take an early morning roundtrip on the Staten Island Ferry for some great views of the Statue of Liberty. Back in the Financial District, pay your respects at Ground Zero (p.51) before heading to Midtown for a free tour of Grand Central Station (www.grandcentralterminal.com). Get sustenance in the form of a slice of genuine New York pizza (around $3), then enjoy a stroll around Central Park (p.204); in summer there may be a free concert in progress. Enjoy a cheap feast (p.216), before heading for Times Square, where you can get yourself a cheesy 'I heart NY' T-shirt (shop around and you'll get five for $10).

For Culture Junkies...

Spend an hour or two in the reading room at the New York Public Library on Fifth Avenue (at 40th Street) – entry is free and you can browse through thousands of books, or just admire the dreamy murals on the ceiling. Enjoy a meal at Fraunces Tavern (p.215) – it was good enough for George Washington and his pals, and features a fascinating historical display. Then head to the Upper East Side (p.104) and make the most of 'Museum Mile', where you'll find the Met (p.108), the Guggenheim (p.107), the Whitney (p.109) and many more within walking distance. Sip a delicate French cognac in Brandy Library Lounge (p.24), before catching an indie flick at the Angelika in Soho (www.angelikafilmcenter.com).

Visiting New York

New York welcomes seven million international visitors each year, and despite tight security, getting into the Big Apple is relatively straightforward.

Getting There

New York City is served by two international airports – JFK in Queens and Newark in New Jersey – and another dedicated to domestic flights only, La Guardia in Queens. Between them, they handle the millions of air passengers that fly into New York every year. JFK is seen as the major point of entry for international travellers.

Everyone landing at JFK must go through passport control, even if they are only there in transit. This inolves a passport check, and you must submit the relevant visa form (p.14), answer a few security questions, have your photo taken (so smile!), and have your fingerprints taken.

Since 9/11, air travel has taken on a new level of seriousness in the US, and you should allow extra time for security checks both before you fly and when you arrive. To get through arrivals faster, it can help to be prepared. You will have to put all your belongings through the scanners, including your shoes – so it will save time if you start taking these off while still in the queue. Laptops have to come out of laptop bags to be scanned separately, and you may have to remove the battery. All jackets and scarves must also be scanned.

Airlines

Aer Lingus	866 886 8844	www.flyaerlingus.com
Air Canada	888 247 2262	www.aircanada.com
Air France	800 237 2747	www.airfrance.us
Alitalia	800 223 5730	www.alitaliausa.com
American Airlines	800 433 7300	www.aa.com
British Airways	800 247 9297	www.britishairways.com
Cathay Pacific	800 233 2742	www.cathaypacific.com
China Airlines	917 368 2000	www.china-airlines.com
Continental Airlines	800 523 3273	www.continental.com
Delta Airlines	800 221 1212	www.delta.com
Emirates	800 777 3999	www.emirates.com
Etihad Airways	888 838 4423	www.etihadairways.com
Gulf Air	888 359 4853	www.gulfairco.com
Lufthansa	800 645 3880	www.lufthansa.com
Malaysia Airlines	212 697 8994	www.malaysiaairlines.com
Northwest Airlines	800 225 2525	www.nwa.com
Qantas Airways	800 227 4500	www.qantas.com
Singapore Airlines	800 742 3333	www.singaporeair.com
South African Airways	800 722 9675	www.flysaa.com
Southwest Airlines	800 435 9792	www.southwest.com
United Airlines	800 864 8331	www.united.com
US Airways	800 428 4322	www.usairways.com
Virgin Atlantic	800 821 5438	www.virgin-atlantic.com

E-tickets and Electronic Check-in

Electronic tickets and check-ins are practically the norm when it comes to travelling within the United States. However, due to customs, passport control and increased security regulations, international flights from New York do not allow electronic check-in, so you've no choice but the check-in queue!

Airport Transport

Catching a cab from any of New York's airports is costly as you have to pay a fixed fare (around $50) as well as road tolls. It's cheaper to take public transport or an airport bus, which will deliver you to your hotel for a fraction of the price of a cab (around $20 one way). Report to the information desk by the Arrivals exit, and pay the driver when he drops you off.

Visas and Customs

Visa requirements for entering the United States vary greatly depending on nationality, so always check regulations before you travel. Non-American citizens need a visa to enter the US – your nationality and your reason for visiting will determine what kind of visa you should apply for.

Visa Waiver Programme (VWP)

The Visa Waiver Programme allows visitors from certain countries (see the list on p.15) to stay in the US for 90 days without having to apply for a visa. It requires visitors to carry machine-readable passports complete with integrated data chip and digital photograph. There are two ways of getting a Visa Waiver; the first is to apply ahead of time to the US embassy or consulate in your home country. The second is to fill out a green I-94 visa waiver form before you hit the immigration desk. The official will ask you a few questions about the length and purpose of your visit, before taking your photo and your fingerprint (everyone has to have this done). You must provide the address of where you will be staying – if you don't fill out that section of the form you will be denied entry, so it is best to be prepared. For more information you can check out the http://travel.state.gov website.

Other Visas

Travellers not on the VWP list must apply for a visa. There are many different visa classifications (you can get a full list from www. unitedstatesvisas.gov). Costs vary – some are free of charge, and only require you to fill out the relevant forms in good time. Others require you to fill out an application and attend an interview at the US consulate in your home country.

VWP Countries

There are currently 27 countries that participate in the Visa Waiver Programme, so citizens of these countries get visas on arrival: Andorra, Australia, Austria, Belgium, Brunei, Denmark, Finland, France, Germany, Iceland, Ireland, Italy, Japan, Liechtenstein, Luxembourg, Monaco, the Netherlands, New Zealand, Norway, Portugal, San Marino, Singapore, Slovenia, Spain, Sweden, Switzerland and the United Kingdom.

Local Knowledge

When travelling, it's best to be prepared – this section covers the essential info that you should know while you are in New York.

You'll find plenty of kiosks throughout the city, doling out handy information on places to go and things to see – but be ready for long queues during busy seasons. These include five official New York City Visitor Information Centers: for their locations check the official NYC website www.nycvisit.com. Or you could head for the Big Apple Visitors' Center on East 86th Street – they can help you plan your trip, come up with a suitable itinerary, and give you some excellent insider tips. Before travelling, you could also check out some of the excellent online resources first. Try www.nycvisit.com or www.nyctourist.com for some excellent tips and tricks for making the most of your stay.

Time

New York is five hours behind UCT (Universal Coordinated Time). However, between the second Sunday in March and the first Sunday of November, daylight savings moves it an hour forward.

Standard office hours are 08:00 to 17:00 or 09:00 to 18:00, Monday to Friday. Public transportation runs 24 hours a day, with less frequent but still well-serviced subway and bus stops, so it's pretty normal to find folk about town even in the wee hours (hence being known as the city that never sleeps).

Shops and department stores tend to keep varying opening hours between 08:00 and 22:00. During major retailing seasons like Christmas or at sale time, the hours may change to stay open for longer.

Climate

New York's climate fits with its Mediterranean latitude, with humidity varying enough to notice throughout the year, and its coastal location and waterways ensuring the place never gets as cold as it does further inland. The seasons here are well defined, with hot and sweaty summers and chilly

Embassies & Consulates	
Austria	212 737 64 00
Canada	212 596 16 28
China	212 244 94 56
Denmark	212 223 45 45
Finland	212 750 44 00
France	212 606 36 88
Germany	212 610 97 00
India	212 774 06 00
Ireland	212 319 25 62
Israel	212 499 56 10
Italy	212 737 91 00
Japan	212 371 82 22
Netherlands	212 246 14 30
New Zealand	212 832 40 38
Norway	212 421 73 33
Philippines	212 764 13 30
Russia	212 348 06 26
South Africa	212 213 48 80
Spain	212 355 40 80
Sweden	212 563 25 50
Switzerland	212 599 57 00
UK	212 745 02 00

winters, so dress accordingly. White Christmases are common, drizzly rains even more so during the winter months. Spring and autumn are pleasant seasons, avoiding the extremes of the bits in between, with mild temperatures and low humidity levels. Before venturing out anywhere, it is always wise to check the latest forecast online or on TV.

Dos and Don'ts

Despite New York being fairly liberal, there are some laws you should definitely not cross. It is illegal to drink alcohol in public places, so if you must carry around a bottle of booze, you are required to have it covered or inside a brown bag (classy). When it comes to smoking – you are not allowed to smoke inside any building, except for your own home. Restaurants, bars and nightclubs are all smoke-free zones, although some may have little smoking balconies where the few remaining smokers can huddle outside for a quickie.

As one of the fashion capitals of the world, nothing is off limits, and nobody stares – New York is the land of the fashion-free! Obviously if you are attending a religious service in a temple, church or mosque, it's respectful to stick to conservative attire and some restaurants have smart dress codes. Your greatest challenge will be dressing appropriately for the weather, which can change in an instant. Sometimes air conditioning can be a bit aggressive, especially in cinemas and on the subway during summer, so an emergency cardigan may come in handy.

Tipping

You have to get used to tipping in New York – it is practically a crime not to tip for most services, even if the service was awful. For a taxi driver, you should tip $1 for a trip costing under $10, $2 for a trip costing $10 to $20, and so on. In a pub or a bar, the rule is $1 to $2 per drink, or more if the drink involved some skillful mixing. You'll often see service deteriorate if your tip is deemed too small, so be prepared to part with the cash if you want your drinks with a dash of speed and a hint of a smile! You should tip your restaurant waiter anything from 15% to 20% (if your maths is bad, just double the tax). A bellhop will expect between $2 and $5 if he helps you with your bags or hails you a cab, and you should leave $2 or $3 per day for your hotel maid. If you are paying by credit card, you just add the tip to the final amount before signing.

Crime and Safety

For a big city, New York is pretty safe – thanks largely to a visible police presence and streets that are generally busy any time of day or night. However, you do need to keep your wits about you; walk with purpose and don't stop to dither over directions or to find your 'cellphone' in the depths of your bag – if you need to stop to check your map, pop into a shop or cafe, get your bearings and head back out onto the street. Keep a firm hold on your bag, and don't make life easy for pickpockets by carrying your wallet in your back pocket.

One last word on crime: beware of scam artists. They say New Yorkers are rude but that's actually untrue. However, with so many scam artists on the prowl, it's best to just avoid eye contact with others and keep on walking if anybody tries to stop and talk to you in the street. Someone who pops out in front of you to ask the time could be distracting you while his mate pickpockets you, and that is just one of the millions of scams out there. So be vigilant and don't fall for any of their tricks. If you do end up being the victim of a crime, give the Crime Victims Hotline a call (212 577 7777).

Police

Endearingly referred to as 'New York's finest', the NYPD (New York Police Department) are vigilant and happy to help – whether you're just in need of directions or you have a genuine emergency. Dressed in dark blue uniforms and characteristic hats, you'll see them on almost every street corner, and even on the subway, which is now part of their patrol. They are armed and take their role seriously, aiming to make the city as safe as possible while still maintaining a friendly demeanour. The official website has lots of useful information, including details of all NYPD precincts, contact information and safety tips (www.nyc.gov/html/nypd). In case you don't spot a cop on the beat, you can also dial 911 (and ask for the police department).

Physically Challenged Visitors

On the whole, the city is well prepared for people with special needs. The Mass Transit System (MTA) in particular has taken great steps to ensure that all passengers are taken care of, including those with physical challenges or special needs. There are Braille maps, large-print maps, elevators and ramps in many subway stops, and a door-to-door para-transit service. Visit www.mta.info or call 800 734 6772 for more information.

Many of the larger hotels, and some restaurants, are built with spacious doorways and corridors, ramps for wheelchair users, and extra services for people with special needs. Busy pedestrian walkways and impatient New Yorkers are perhaps the biggest hindrance, especially during rush hour when the sidewalks take on an 'every man for himself' aggression.

Money

The monetary unit is the dollar ($), which is divided into 100 cents. All notes are the same colour (green), no matter what denomination – making it somewhat tricky for tourists to tell the difference between bills at first. Coins come in denominations of one dollar, 25 cents (also called a quarter), 10 cents (a dime), five cents (a nickel) and one cent (a penny).

Cash may be king, but New York is one of the shopping capitals of the world, and as long as you can pay, you can do it any way you like. Credit cards are accepted in all but a handful of smaller shops or market stalls – although in many cases there is a minimum spend requirement (usually $10), or a surcharge (usually around $1.50). Otherwise, there are no other charges for paying by card. Some hotels require a credit card as guarantee, even if you intend to settle your final bill with cash. Nearly all restaurants accept cash or card, and you can even buy your subway Metrocard using your credit card.

Cheques and travellers' cheques are a bit more tricky – you won't find many places that accept cheques without asking questions, and travellers' cheques need to be converted, which can be time consuming. New York is one of the most international cities in the world, but that doesn't mean you can use foreign currency here – if you are paying cash, then you'll need good old American dollars.

Banks

A strong network of banks includes all the major American and international names, each with several branches around the city. To find a particular bank's nearest branch, it is best to check on their website – not only will you find out branch locations, but also what services are available at each branch (like whether there is a customer service desk or an ATM). Opening hours vary, but they are generally 08:00 to 17:00, Monday to Friday.

You're never far away from an ATM in New York – you'll find one in most banks, but also in many supermarkets, delis, hotel lobbies and even some bars. ATMs in locations other than banks charge you a minimum of $1.50 for every transaction. Every ATM will display symbols of the financial networks that are accepted, such as Cirrus, Visa, Visa Electron, Plus and MasterCard. Often, an ATM will only let you withdraw a minimum of $20, and many also have maximum daily withdrawal amounts, which varies from bank to bank.

Money Exchanges

Unfortunately money exchange is a fairly complicated affair, with many major banks only offering the service for their own customers. There are random exchange offices (or bureaux de change) around town, but these usually give lousy rates or charge high commission. One solution is to use your credit card or ATM card to withdraw dollars. If you do need to exchange money, try to do it at the airport or at well-known offices like Thomas Cook (at various locations).

Electricity & Water

The United States runs on 110V at 60Hz, so you'll need a converter since the rest of the world runs much higher at 220/240 Volts 50 Cycles (50HZ). American plugs have two parallel flat blades above a circular grounding pin. The alternative is a plug that is just two parallel flat blades.

The Safe Water Drinking Act has ensured that New York has the best quality water facilities. It's safe to drink straight from the tap, but it's also very much a culture that finds swilling from schmancy bottles de rigueur, so it's your call.

Telephone and Internet

New York's public telephones can still be found on almost every corner, and a four minute call within the city will cost you a quarter, or $1 for a national call. Some take phone cards, some just coins (usually no pennies, so keep copper in your pocket); just look at the front of the phone to find out whether it takes cards or coins. Public telephones do break down: it is estimated that one in five public phones are on the blink at any time, but they are a good resource nevertheless, especially if you are not travelling with a mobile phone.

When phoning internationally, it can work out cheaper to buy a card from any bodega, deli or cornershop – shop around, because some are cheaper than others for certain countries or regions.

Internet access is very easy to come by, with many places such as cafes offering free wireless access (buy a latte for good karma points). You'll struggle to find a branch of Starbucks, Barnes & Noble or McDonalds that doesn't offer

Wi-Fi (although in rare cases there may be a charge). You can walk into the Apple Store on Fifth Avenue for free WiFi, and if you are not travelling with a laptop you can even use one of their demo models. There are also internet cafes such as Cybercafe (250 W. 49th Street, 212 333 4109; www.cyber-cafe.com) or the massive easyInternetcafe (234 West 42nd Street; www.easyinternetcafe.com), which boasts over 600 PCs and is the largest internet cafe in the world.

Lost and Found

If you have anything stolen, you should report the incident to the police as soon as possible. Either dial 911 (emergency service and ask for police department) or stop a cop, which is easy to do, as they are everywhere and super helpful. You will have to file a police report on anything that's been taken, especially if you're hoping to make a claim with your insurance company.

Should you lose your travel documents, the first thing to do is to file a police report. Then get in touch with your embassy or consulate (see the list on p.17) as soon as possible. As a precaution though, you should always make sure you have copies of your important documents stored separately from them.

If you lose your credit card, contact your bank as soon as you can so that they can block it. Once you've reported the loss, you will not be liable for any further transactions made on your card.

Viewfinder on top of the Empire State Building

TURN
TO CLEAR
VISION

QUARTERS ONLY

U.S. Manufactured
and Distributed by
THE TOWER OPTICAL COMPANY, INC.

$ .50 ¢

TO OPERATE
TURN
HANDLE
ONE
FULL
TURN

Further Information

Local media is a great source of information on current events: this section tells you what to look out for, as well as how to send that postcard home or where to go when nature calls.

Newspapers & Magazines

There are over 40 daily newspapers available in New York, with the locally published US papers being the Wall Street Journal, the New York Times, the New York Daily News and the New York Post. Newspapers can be bought at paper stands on streets, from vending machines, bookshops or subway stations. The average price of a broadsheet is $1.25, although Sunday editions can cost a bit more ($2.00). Bookshops and larger paper stands sell international and foreign language newspapers and magazines. Several weekly newspapers are useful for visitors: The Village Voice comes out on Wednesdays and you can get your free copy from red boxes on street corners (www.villagevoice.com). The L Magazine (www.thelmagazine.com) includes info on Brooklyn, so if you plan to explore this fascinating borough, pick up a copy.

Websites

Try www.nycvisit.com or www.nyc.gov – both sites are excellent for tourist information. If you need some nightlife info, www.timeout.com/newyork or www.nymag.com (New York Magazine's online edition) have all the info on bars, restaurants, cinema, comedy and theatre, as well as reviews. Another great online resource is Shecky's (www.sheckys.com).

Postal Services

The US Postal Service (www.usps.com) is one of the world's best. The service is incredibly reliable and they are always coming up with ways to make things run even more smoothly. If you wish to post a letter or a postcard, you can buy stamps from post offices, grocery stores and tourist gift shops, and you'll find a post box (dark blue in colour) on just about every street corner.

Public Toilets

There are few toilets actually open to the public in New York. Public conveniences can be found in Grand Central Terminal rail station, Port Authority Bus Terminal and in the city's parks. If you find yourself in need in a department store or hotel, you should take the opportunity to visit the quality facilities there. Other than that, try fast food restaurants and coffee shops, and search for the toilets inside (try to act like a customer!), which are usually kept in excellent condition.

Residents' Reviews
One of the most popular guides in the city is the Zagat Guide, which represents feedback received from thousands of New Yorkers on some of the best restaurants, bars and nightclubs in the city (www.zagat.com).

Getting Around

Getting around in New York is no problem – you can take the subway, hop on a bus, hail an iconic yellow cab, or simply put on your most comfortable shoes and explore the city on foot.

Once you get your bearings, New York is one of the easiest cities in the world to navigate, with a complex yet superlative network to get you from Avenue A to the Bronx. The grid system means that you should be able to find your way around effortlessly (street numbers increase northwards, while the numbers on avenues run east to west). With every street lined with great shops, interesting history and beautiful sights, New York is an amazing city to explore on foot.

The public transport system is excellent, and consists of a network of buses, boats, the subway and trains that most residents depend upon. Public transport is operated by the MTA (Mass Transit Authority, www.mta.info), and runs throughout the day and night in all areas of the city, including the boroughs.

Classic yellow New York taxi cabs are everywhere and very handy – although they are most prolific in Manhattan. They are cheap and hailing one is pretty easy once you've learnt a few tips and tricks (and as long as it's not raining, when it's nearly impossible to find an available cab).

Boat

The Staten Island Ferry is the busiest in the United States, carrying millions of people between Manhattan and Staten Island. Since 1997, this ferry has been free, making it one of the best bargains in New York. Even if you don't need to go to Staten Island, it's still worth taking the trip for amazing views of the Statue of Liberty and the New York skyline. There are several other boat services, such as the Water Taxi (www.nywatertaxi.com) which stops at 10 places around the city, NY Waterway (www.nywaterway.com), and the Circle Line Ferry (www.circlelinedowntown.com).

Bus

Although not quite as popular as the subway, a fleet of nearly 6,000 buses works 300 routes around the city. Bus stops are clearly marked and always within walking distance. A one-way journey will cost you $2.00, and you need the exact money as the drivers don't give change. For fuss-free travel, pick up a MetroCard (pay for a daily, weekly or monthly pass) at any subway station to allow you access to the subway and bus network.

The Port Authority Bus Terminal (625 Eighth Ave, between Eighth and Ninth Avenues and 40th to 42nd street) is the central stop for all the buses, including services that take you beyond the five boroughs. You can also catch the national Greyhound and Peter Pan buses from here.

Car

New York is not a car-friendly city – only a third of New Yorkers actually own a car – as some areas get really congested, finding street parking can be a nightmare and parking garages cost astronomical amounts. With the excellent public transport network, you'll not have any trouble getting around without your own wheels.

If you're planning on heading out of the city, hiring a car is easy with all major international chains represented both at the airport and at various locations around the city. With virtually all companies, you can book your car online and pay by credit card – in fact, most car hire companies will require credit card details as a guarantee, so have the plastic ready. Rates can start as low as $75 per week for a standard car, or you can treat yourself to something flashier for $50 per day and upwards. Driving is on the right side of the road, and petrol prices are cheaper than many other countries.

When you return the car, make sure the tank is full or you'll pay a gas surcharge. All reputable car hire companies will do a thorough, multi-point check on the car, inside and out, while you are present – this is to check for existing damage and is for your own protection. The last thing you need is to be charged for a scratch that was on the car long before you got in it. It is also wise to take the extra insurance – even the tiniest scratch on a hire car will cost you big bucks. Also if you are planning an epic roadtrip, Kerouac-style, make sure that you are permitted to take your hired car out of state – often the small print says otherwise.

Car Rental Agencies

AAMCAR	212 927 7000	www.aamcar.com
Accessible Vans of America	800 282 8297	www.accessiblevans.com
Alamo	800 462 5266	www.alamo.com
Avis	800 331 1212	www.avis.com
Budget	800 527 0700	www.budgetrentacar.com
Dollar Rent A Car	800 800 4000	www.dollarcar.com
Enterprise Rent-A-Car	800 325 8007	www.enterprise.com
Hertz	800 654 3131	www.hertz.com
National Car Rental	800 227 7638	www.nationalcar.com
New York Rent-A-Car	212 799 1100	www.ny-car.com

Subway

The New York Subway (www.mta.info) is one of the largest underground train systems in the world, and is used by billions of people each year. It is safe, easy to navigate (once you get the hang of it), and it can be pretty entertaining, thanks to a large variety of 'travelling' musicians, poets and artists riding along with you, hoping for a bit of spare change. Even if there is no entertainment, a ride on the subway is a great way to get up close with the people of New York, who are an eclectic bunch!

To ride the subway, all you need to do is get yourself a ticket. Every subway station has a ticket office or a vending machine – the vending machines are a quick way to get your subway pass: you just pop in the amount required (some machines give change), follow the instructions on screen, and you'll get a plastic card with a magnetic strip that you just swipe at the turnstiles. A one-way ride (no matter what distance) costs $2, but you can get a one-day pass giving you unlimited rides for $7. A seven-day unlimited ride pass costs $24 and a 30 day unlimited ride pass costs $76. Reduced fares are available for people over 65 and those with certain disabilities.

The subway is not just a handy way to get around – it is also as much an experience of New York as Times Square or Central Park. Apart from the great people-watching possibilities, spending time underground can improve your appreciation of music: the MTA sponsors a music programme whereby it pays over 100 musicians to perform at various locations each week. Some are talented and some just have to be seen to be believed – if you can find her, check out the 'saw lady' – Natalia Paruz plays a long bendy saw to create a melancholic yet beautiful sound (www.sawlady.com).

Taxi

New York's yellow cabs are one of the most recognisable icons of the city. There are over 13,000 yellow cabs as well as over 40,000 other taxis, mini cabs and limo services. Yellow cabs are the only ones permitted to pick up passengers hailing from the street, although others will try to do so. When hailing a cab, try to flag down those with their roof lights on – if the light is off it means the cab is already occupied or the driver is off duty. All cabs are non-smoking. It is highly recommended (and required by law) to fasten your seatbelt during your journey.

All yellow cabs are metered and a journey starts at $2.50, although this goes up to $3.00 after 20:00 and $3.50 during the peak hours between 16:00 and 20:00. The meter ticks up every one-fifth of a mile, or every two minutes if you're stuck in traffic. You should always, always tip the driver. There are no rules on how much, but generally you should tip $1 for a trip costing under $10, $2 for a trip costing $10 to $20, and so on.

Walking

Walking is one of the most popular ways to get around the city. Things can get pretty congested at times and there is a definite 'street code' to follow, so don't dawdle along or suddenly stop in the middle of the pavement to take a photo of something. But on the whole, walking around helps you 'feel' more of the city – the sights, the sounds, the smells and the collective heartbeat of all the New Yorkers on the streets.

Before you buy that subway ticket, check on a map how far it really is between where you are and where you're going. In many cases, walking doesn't take that much longer than going underground. The grid system of the streets makes it really easy to figure out where you're walking to, until you get into Soho, and only then things get more confusing. However, once you get below Houston Street and the grid system disappears, your feet are often the best mode of transport anyway, since the streets are congested and not even the most determined cab driver can beat the traffic in Soho and the Financial District.

Places to Stay

From a bunkbed in an art gallery to a shower with a view or even a goldfish for company, New York's hotels are anything but standard.

New York welcomes thousands of guests every day, from every corner of the world and with every size wallet – from the two-penny rubbers to the mightier clientele with deeper pockets. Hence the city's accommodation structure: you'll find all sorts here from five star to five in a room, and from boutique chic to bunk beds.

New York City certainly has its fair share of hotels. Most are in Manhattan, but it's just as easy, and usually much, much cheaper, to venture out into the boroughs. Certain neighbourhoods, like the theatre district and Times Square, tend to be cluttered. Expect to fork out a handsome sum for the more upscale hotels, and if you're adamant on staying in Manhattan, you'll find some fairly outrageous prices where the service and standards just don't seem to match.

Prices start at around $150 per night, and this can go up to $750 and well beyond if you are looking for real luxury. Some hotels have amenities straight out of a Hollywood fantasy, like chefs that will come to your room to prepare dinner and free club entries. One way to try getting more luxury for your dollar is to log onto travel deal websites like www.expedia.com or www.lastminute.com, where you can sometimes get fancy hotels at bargain prices (you have to have luck on your side though).

Waldorf=Astoria

Just because you are paying a lot doesn't mean you are guaranteed luxury or even hygiene. If you do find yourself in a sorry hotel situation, speak up and don't settle for sub-standard accommodation.

For a more personal experience, while guesthouses are often no cheaper than hotels, they have fewer rooms, congenial staff and a pleasant family atmosphere. The very cheapest places to stay are the hostels – no longer restricted to hard-up students or bearded travellers, you can pay a fraction of the price of a hotel, as long as you don't mind sharing in close quarters with other people. They can also be a great place to meet people to share your New York experiences with.

60 Thompson
www.thompsonhotels.com
877 431 0400
With only a hundred rooms, this Soho boutique hotel is tranquil and exclusive, and one of the most stylish hotels around. The beautiful rooms come complete with Fresh bath products and a Dean & Deluca Pantry.

The Algonquin
www.algonquinhotel.com
212 840 6800
This hotel, located in the heart of the city, has a history that is as fascinating as it is long, and encapsulates the heart and soul of old New York. It's classy, from its 'old money' decor to its pampered house cat, Matilda.

Casablanca Hotel
www.casablancahotel.com
212 869 1212
This tranquil haven of Moroccan splendour is based largely on the classic film of the same name, and is set amid the madness of Times Square. Snuggle up by the fireplace in Rick's Cafe for a cosy end to any day.

Gershwin Hotel
www.gershwinhotel.com
212 545 8000
Doubling as an art gallery, with the beauty inside and the amazing area of New York outside, this is one hotel you'll want to linger in longer. A bunkbed will set you back just $40 per night.

Gramercy Park Hotel
www.gramercyparkhotel.com
212 920 3300
Full of oversized artworks and contemporary minimalism, with all guest suites individually decorated, this is one of the most stylish stopovers in the city. The penthouse is the definition of luxurious opulence.

The Hotel Chelsea
www.hotelchelsea.com
212 243 3700
Calling itself 'a rest stop for rare individuals', the privacy and calm of the hotel is a hotbed for creativity and a magnet for bohemia. Every room looks different, and a single room starts from under $200.

Hotel Gansevoort
www.hotelgansevoort.com
212 206 6700
Stunning views, full-service luxury, stylish surroundings and its location in the Meatpacking District make this hotel a destination of choice for stylistas, the uber cool and celebrities. Amenities include an exclusive spa and rooftop pool.

Hotel on Rivington
www.hotelonrivington.com
212 475 2600
This award-winning hotel is basically a 21 storey glass tower on the Lower East Side, with unobstructed, panoramic views of the Manhattan skyline. Even some of the showers have views to die for.

Jumeirah Essex House
www.jumeirahessexhouse.com
212 247 0300
First built in the 1930s, this luxurious hotel is spread over 44 floors and offers amazing views over Central Park and Manhattan. The hotel is conveniently close to major attractions like Times Square, Lincoln Center, Museum Mile and Carnegie Hall.

Mercer Hotel
www.mercerhotel.com
212 966 6060
With its understated luxury making this hotel special, the Mercer has 75 rooms, each decorated to match its majestic Romanesque exterior. Indulge in an in-room beauty treatment or order from the 24 hour room service menu to complete your stay.

Morgans Hotel
www.morganshotel.com
212 686 0300
Located in the heart of swanky Manhattan, Morgans is credited as being New York's very first boutique hotel and is always in demand. With chic yet welcoming decor, the hotel is a temple of comfort and style.

Roosevelt Hotel
www.theroosevelthotel.com
212 661 9600
Over 80 years old, but not showing its age at all, the luxurious rooms and legendary service are good reasons to choose this landmark hotel. The convenient location is a huge draw – walk to the Met, the Rockefeller Center or the Empire State Building.

Soho Grand
www.sohogrand.com
212 965 3000
Modelled on the much sought-after Soho-style lofts, the comfortable rooms have huge windows offering great views of the New York skyline. Feeling lonely? Here you can order a pet goldfish to lift your spirits, at no extra cost!

Trump International Hotel
www.trumpintl.com
212 299 1000
Perfect for the well-heeled business traveller, the luxurious suites offer awesome skyline views over Central Park. It's also the home of famous French restaurant Jean Georges (p.235).

Waldorf=Astoria
www.waldorf.com
212 355 3000
From the gorgeous art deco design to the seamless service, this tower of luxury has captured the hearts of guests for well over a hundred years.

Guesthouses

Guesthouses and bed and breakfasts are plentiful in the city, with the cosier options located in the Lower East Side, Tribeca, Soho and Brooklyn. Amenities usually include free internet, cable TV and in-room telephone as well as continental breakfasts. Abingdon Guest House (www.abingdonhouse.com) takes up two adjoining brownstones in the West Village and is tastefully decorated and professionally run. The East Village Bed & Coffee (www.bedandcoffee.com) has individually themed rooms and some funky common areas.

Hostels

The best value accommodation in the city – you'll find some very decent, very safe and very clean hostels that offer dorm-style or even private rooms. Almost all hostels have shared bathrooms, but it's the only downside to some very funky little places for very cheap rates. The YMCA (www.ymcanyc. org) has a number of hostels throughout Manhattan, but the Vanderbilt hostel (212 912 2500) on the Upper East Side is particularly good – the location and price are phenomenal, but you'll have to book well in advance as demand is high.

Hostels

Broadway Hotel & Hostel	212 244 7827	www.broadwayhotelnyc.coma
Hostelling International	212 932 2300	www.hinewyork.org
Hotel 31	212 685 3060	www.hotel31.com
The Portland Square Hotel	212 382 0600	www.portlandsquarehotel.com
Wanderers Inn West	212 222 5602	www.wanderersinn.com

Public Holidays & Annual Events

Someone is always celebrating in New York, and you can join in the party by timing your visit right.

Public Holidays

Public holidays here are mostly either religious holidays (Christmas and Easter among the more celebrated) or patriotic anniversaries such as Independence Day and the Thanksgiving Day parade. There are a couple of just-for-fun days like Gay Pride (a lot of fun, whatever your orientation), Groundhog Day and, of course, the world-famous Halloween Parade.

Just because it's a holiday doesn't necessarily mean everyone's off. Public and government bodies as well as banks are more likely to be closed, but the private sector is more than likely to be toiling away through many of these, with workers joining in the fun after having punched in a full day's slog.

Public Holidays	
New Year's Day	Jan 1
Martin Luther King's Day	3rd Mon in Jan
President's Day	3rd Mon in Feb
Memorial Day	Last Mon in May
Independence Day	July 4
Labor Day	1st Mon in Sep
Columbus Day	2nd Mon in May
Veterans Day	Nov 11
Thanksgiving	4th Thu in Nov
Christmas Day	Dec 25

Financial District

Annual Events
Throughout the year you'll see New Yorkers marching down Fifth Avenue or crowding into Times Square to join together in celebration. These are some of the major annual events that you should definitely consider when planning the dates for your trip. Keep an eye on local press and New York websites for more information and confirmed dates.

Restaurant Week
January & June

Twice a year the city's finest restaurants slash their prices for a week – you're looking at around $24 for a fixed lunch menu, and $35 for dinner (miraculously low, given the usual prices). Keep your eyes on local websites or press for details.

Museum Mile Festival
June

www.museummilefestival.org
On the second Tuesday in June, 23 blocks along Fifth Avenue are closed to traffic and filled with live musicians, street performers, dancing, and general fun. Plus, entrance to the nine museums along that strip is free for the day.

Christmas Tree Lighting Ceremony
November

www.rockefellercenter.com
The lighting up of the famous Christmas tree at the Rockefeller Center marks the start of the holiday season. It is televised and features performances by the Radio City Rockettes. It's not just any old tree – it is usually around 65 feet tall and 35 feet wide.

Macy's Thanksgiving Day Parade   November
www.macys.com
Undoubtedly the city's biggest parade, this event kicks off at
09:00 (but you'll need to be there much earlier) from Central
Park and heads through Times Square on to Macy's, and
features giant animated characters. Dress warmly.

New Year's Eve   December
The Times Square New Year's Eve celebrations are world
famous and something you should do at least once! Gather
with thousands of other shivering revellers to watch the
crystal ball drop and ring in the new year.

New York Fashion Week   February & September
Twice a year, the fashion glitterati and limo-loads of
celebrities descend on New York in a frenzied torrent of tutus
and cashmere as the city plays host to these gurus of style to
drool over next season's 'must-haves'.

New York Film Festival   September/October
www.filmlinc.com
This film festival doesn't award any prizes, but showcases a
selection of 28 feature films and 12 short films selected by a
committee of experts. Book your tickets early online.

New York Jazz Festival   June
www.festivalproductions.net
The New York jazz scene is one of the best in the world, and
thus the New York Jazz Festival is one of the most hotly

Essentials

Public Holidays & Annual Events

anticipated events on the musical calendar – a two-week
celebration of everything that makes jazz cool.

New York Marathon
November

www.nycmarathon.org

The largest marathon in the world, a whopping 90,000
athletes took to the streets on the course through the five
boroughs of New York in 2006.

St Patrick's Day
17th March

Even if you are not even slightly Irish, when the city turns
green for a day, the atmosphere is electric and everybody is
welcome. The grand St Patrick's Day Parade, which heads up
Fifth Avenue, is a huge affair.

Tribeca Film Festival
May

www.tribecafilmfestival.org

The Tribeca Film Festival showcases an impressive
range of international blockbusters, independent works,
documentaries and family-friendly films during the first week
of May. Book very early to get tickets.

US Open Tennis Championships

www.usopen.org
August/September

This is the final event in the Grand Slam Tournament. All the
big names turn out to fight for the champion's trophy, and
you'll have to be on the ball to get your tickets before they all
sell out.

View from the Top of the Rock, at the Rockefeller Center

Exploring

Explore New York

For a city as huge as New York, it's surprisingly easy to get around. And get around you should; each area has a unique personality just waiting to be explored.

New York is one of the easiest cities to navigate, all thanks to the street grid system, which was devised way back in the early 1800s. Street numbers increase northwards, while avenues run east to west with the numbers increasing westwards. With every street lined with great shops, interesting history and beautiful sights, New York is an amazing city to explore on foot.

That said, if your feet get tired you can make use of the excellent public transport system – a network of buses and the subway can get you wherever you need to go. All public transport is operated by the Metropolitan Transit Authority (MTA), and runs 24 hours a day. Of course, classic yellow New York taxi cabs are everywhere and come in very handy. They are cheap, and hailing one is pretty easy – just as long as its not raining, when finding an empty cab is nearly impossible.

Perhaps a good place to start exploring the city is from Central Park – this green lung of Manhattan is a marvellous place to spend a few hours. It is banked by the Upper East Side (p.104) and the Upper West Side (p.112), both affluent areas with quiet streets, classy apartment buildings and posh restaurants.

Just south of Central Park is the Midtown area (p.84), where you will find many of New York's famous attractions. It is extremely busy during the daytime, and is a great destination for shopping and exploring. To the south-west of Midtown is Chelsea (p.54), the unofficial gay capital of New York and home to a quirky range of restaurants and galleries. East of Chelsea you'll find the leafy suburb of Gramercy Park (p.72) and the Flatiron District (p.72), named after the iconic, triangular-shaped building at the intersection of 23rd Street, Fifth Avenue and Broadway.

South of 14th Street, the grid system ends and it can be harder to find your way around without a map. West Village (p.118) and East Village (p.60) are worth exploring, particularly for the non-stop entertainment scene. Spend a day or two exploring the areas of Soho and Tribeca (p.98), and the Lower East Side and Chinatown, all of which are as interesting as they are diverse.

Finally, the Financial District is the financial heartbeat of the city and also the location of the 9/11 terrorist attacks. Pay your respects at Ground Zero – although it's largely just a construction site now, there is still a moving display of photographs, a fascinating timeline, a monument to those who died, and the occasional sprig of flowers tied to the fence. The Financial District is also home to Century 21, a bargain-shopper's paradise, and of course Wall Street, where millions of dollars are made and lost every day.

From the Financial District you can walk over Brooklyn Bridge, catch the Staten Island Ferry, or simply head back north up Manhattan and catch all the things you missed on the way down!

At A Glance

Don't be overwhelmed by this dazzling city – you can see it all, and more, if you just read on…

Chelsea & The Meatpacking District

Chelsea has long attracted artists, musicians, and New York's colourful gay population. Right next door, the Meatpacking District has a thing or two to show you about the art of partying.

In the 1990s the Meatpacking District was transformed from a collection of dingy butcher shops to a trendsetting neighbourhood... with a few remaining butcher shops. There are plenty of upscale bars, restaurants, and shops ready to contain the crowds of thirtysomething singles ready to mingle every Saturday night. Those rusty old railroad tracks overhead are the remnants of the long-defunct High Line (www.thehighline.org), soon to become a public park, thanks to the lobbying efforts of a group of 'interested people'. The plan has already inspired a boom in condo construction and attracted the attention of a few cultural institutions eager to move.

Neighbourhood fixture Florent (69 Gansevoort Street at Washington Street, 212 989 5779) has been around for many years now, and it's still a great place to eat and drink 24/7. Bistro Pastis on Ninth Avenue at Little West 12th Street (p.200), while overrun on weekend evenings, is great for weekday breakfast or lunch or for the more exotic, Fatty Crab (643 Hudson Street at Gansevoort Street, 212 352 3590) has great Asian-fusion plates, as does Spice Market on West 13th Street at Ninth Avenue (p.199).

Chelsea was long a gay enclave, but now it is best known

30th Street
Terminal

West 32nd St

West 30th St

Eleventh Avenue

West 28th St

CHELSEA

East 27th St

Chelsea Park

West 24th St

West 25th St

Hudson
River Park

Dia Centre
for Arts

West 20th St

Chelsea Piers

West 34th St

West 33rd St

Ninth Avenue

General Post Office

West 30th St

West 29th St

West 26th St

West 25th St

West 23rd St

West 22nd St

General Theological
Seminary

West 21st St

West 19th St

Tenth Avenue

West 17th St

Ninth Avenue

West 18th St

Eighth Avenue

34th St
Penn Station

Nelson
Tower

1 Penn
Plaza

34th St

New York
Penn Station

Madison
Square
Garden

West 31st St

Eighth Avenue

West 29th St

28th St

Fashion Institute
of Technology

Seventh Avenue

23rd St

The Hotel Chelsea

23rd St

West 22nd St

West 20th St

West 17th St

Joe Dimaggio Highway

Eleventh Avenue

**MEATPACKING
DISTRICT**

Little West 12th St

150m

N

Gansevoort St

Hgratio St

Hotel
Gansevoort

Chelsea
Market

West 15th St

West 14th St

14th St

8th Ave

14th St

Jackson Square

Greenwich Ave

14th St

West 13th St

St Vincent's
Hospital

A

for its 200 art galleries and cluster of high profile nightclubs like Crobar (530 West 28th Street at Tenth Avenue, 212 629 9000), Marquee on Tenth Avenue at West 27th Street (p.201) and Bungalow 8, also on Tenth Avenue (p.424). To work out, ice skate, hit golf balls, and otherwise engage in a bit of athleticism, visit the vast sports complex at Chelsea Piers (Pier 60, www.chelseapiers.com).

The city's best place to buy art books is Printed Matter (195 Tenth Avenue at 22nd Street), and all things photo-related should come from the vast inventory of B&H Photo (420 Ninth Avenue at 33rd Street). As for refreshments and re-energising, Cookshop (156 Tenth Avenue at 20th Street, 212 924 4440) is a wonderful place for cocktails and large portions of well-prepared, seasonal comfort food, La Luncheonette (130 Tenth Avenue at 18th Street, 212 675 0342) and The Red Cat (227 Tenth Avenue at 23rd Street, 212 242 1122) are local standbys, and RUB BBQ (208 West 23rd Street at Seventh Avenue, 212 524 4300) can be counted on for hearty, all-American grub.

For beautiful people, or those looking for them, the Japanese restaurant Ono (p.200) in the Hotel Gansevoort, is a must. The

Hotel Chic

The notorious Chelsea Hotel (p. 37) has hosted Jimi Hendrix, Janis Joplin, and Andy Warhol, among others. The architecturally intriguing Maritime Hotel (363 West 16th Street) has a fabulous facade and a couple of restaurants and bars that draw crowds to party on its spacious terrace. And then of course there's the Gansevoort (p.38), where you'll find all the pretty people and bucketloads of celebrities.

hotel itself is a magnet for stylistas, the uber cool, celebrities and the wealthy (although various package rates do take the sting out of the prices somewhat).

Chelsea Market
Ninth Avenue between 15th and 16th Street
Chelsea Market (www.chelseamarket.com) is packed with edible treats including meats, veggies, sweets and chocolate, wine, cheese and the many delights at the various cosy cafes. Try the brownies from Fat Witch Bakery (888 419 4824), situated inside the market, but be prepared to return before your trip's end. Map A **1**

Chelsea Art Galleries
Various locations
With more than 200 galleries occupying an area less than one square mile in size, Chelsea has the world's highest concentration of art dealers. The majority of galleries can be found between 20th and 26th Streets from Tenth to Eleventh Avenues, with the most crowded streets being 22nd, 24th, and 25th Streets. Some notable local galleries are Andrea Rosen (525 West 24th Street), Exit Art (475 Tenth Avenue), Friedrich Petzel (535 West 22nd Street), Bellwether (134 Tenth Avenue), Gagosian Gallery (555 West 24th Street), Mary Boone (541 West 24th Street), Matthew Marks (522 West 22nd Street), and Dia: Chelsea (548 West 22nd Street). To visit many galleries in one place, try the Starrett-Lehigh Building (601 West 26th Street) or 529 West 20th Street.

If you only do one thing in...
Chelsea & The Meatpacking District

Sip a cosmopolitan and soak up the sophisticated, speakeasy vibe in the Meatpacking District.

Best for...

Eating: Enjoy stylish Japanese fare in Ono (p.200), preferably alfresco in the bamboo gardens.

Drinking: Order a drink and mingle with celebrities in Tenjune (p.202).

Sightseeing: Spend a few dreamy hours musing over beautiful art in one of Chelsea's many art galleries (p.55).

Shopping: Load up on luxurious goodies and imported delicacies at the Chelsea market (p.55).

Outdoor: Head for the piers in Hudson River Park (www.hudsonriverpark.org) to watch the sunset.

East Village

While it's always been a haven for artists, today the East Village is a bohemian refuge for all walks of life. A vibrant bar scene is the ideal opportunity to mingle with some of life's colourful characters.

The East Village is much more recently gentrified, so it still has a bit of an edge to it – or maybe that's just old graffiti left up on the walls for old times' sake. Tompkins Square Park is the local hub for dog walking, people gawking, and any other outdoor pursuit. Historic St-Mark's-in-the-Bowery Church (131 East 10th Street at Second Avenue) is a community centre of sorts, hosting lectures, poetry readings, and local meetings and New York Theatre Workshop (79 East 4th Street at Second Avenue) and The Public Theatre (425 Lafayette Street at Astor Place) are two of the best places in the city to see staged works. Cinephiles must not skip the Anthology Film Archives (32 Second Avenue at 2nd Street). KGB Bar (85 East 4th Street at First Avenue) has a Soviet theme and a renowned reading series. Many believe that the Nuyorican Poets Café (236 East 3rd Street at Avenue C) is the birthplace of slam poetry, and it is certainly a great place to experience performances by local artists. The honest-to-goodness landmark here is the fully restored home at Merchant's House (29 East 4th Street at Lafayette Street).

Vegans and vegetarians will find many options here, including long-time favourites Angelica Kitchen (300 East

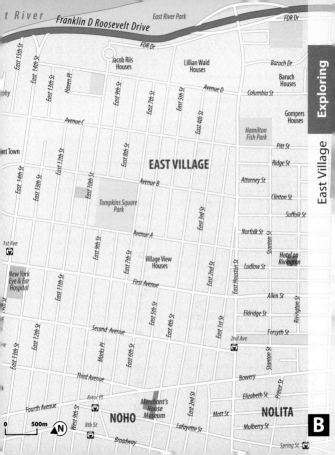

t River

Franklin D Roosevelt Drive

East River Park

FDR Dr

FDR Dr

East 15th St

East 14th St

East 13th St

Hoven Pl

Jacob Riis
Houses

East 9th St

East 7th St

East 5th St

Lillian Wald
Houses

Avenue D

Baruch Dr

Baruch
Houses

Columbia St

Gompers
Houses

Avenue C

East 4th St

Hamilton
Fish Park

Pitt St

nt Town

East 12th St

EAST VILLAGE

Ridge St

East 14th St

East 13th St

East 10th St

Avenue B

Attorney St

Clinton St

Suffolk St

Tompkins Square
Park

East 3rd St

Norfolk St

Stanton St

Avenue A

1st Ave

East 9th St

East 7th St

Village View
Houses

East 2nd St

East Houston St

Ludlow St

Hotel on
Rivington

New York
Eye & Ear
Hospital

East 11th St

First Avenue

Allen St

East 5th St

East 4th St

Eldridge St

Rivington St

East 1st St

East 12th St

Second Avenue

Marks Pl

East 6th St

2nd Ave

Forsyth St

East 13th St

Third Avenue

Bowery

Stanton St

Fourth Avenue

Astor Pl

Merchant's
House
Museum

Elizabeth St

Prince St

West 9th St

NOHO

East 2nd St

NOLITA

500m

N

8th St

Lafayette St

Mott St

Mulberry St

Broadway

Spring St

B

12th Street at Second Avenue, 212 228 2909) and Kate's Joint (58 Avenue B at 4th Street, 212 777 7059). Café Mogador (101 St Mark's Place at First Avenue, 212 677 2226) is a cosy place with simple Moroccan food, especially nice for breakfasts. Candlelit Italian bistro Il Bagatto (192 East 2nd Street at Avenue B, 212 228 3703) is great for a date, and Momofuku (163 First Avenue at 10th Street, www.momofuku.com) is a delicious choice for nights that run late. If it gets really late, Ukranian/Polish diner Velselka (144 Second Avenue at 9th Street, 212 228 9682) is open 24 hours for eastern European snacks and pancakes for breakfast.

Aside from the garish gift kiosks on St Mark's Place, the East Village has become a pleasant place to boutique shop, with plenty of vintage and new clothing for sale. Used book buyers must hit The Strand (828 Broadway at 12th Street), while all the latest academic publications find their way to St Mark's Bookshop (31 Third Avenue at Stuyvesant Place). Veniero's (342 East 11th Street at Second Avenue, 212 674 7070) has been churning out noteworthy cannoli since 1894,

Bar Stop

There are so many bars in the East Village, but one of the best is McSorley's on 7th Street at Third Avenue – it has been in business since 1854, making it the city's oldest continuously operating saloon. There is sawdust on the floor and the drink options are 'dark' or 'light' draft beer, both served two mugs at a time. Women had to sue to gain entry in 1970, and you don't have a hope of getting in on St Patrick's Day.

not a bad buy if Brooklyn's Italian neighbourhoods are just too far away. Venerable bath and body shop Kiehl's (109 Third Avenue at 13th Street) has its flagship store here, so stop in and ask for plenty of free samples. That pear tree out front is a historic reproduction of sorts; a tree stood on that spot from the days when this land was Dutch Colonial Governor Peter Stuyvesant's farm, only to be destroyed by an errant carriage in the 19th century. Kiehl's planted a new one in 2003, and hopefully modern drivers will be more careful.

East Village literally never stops. While some other areas of the city clear out during the summer months (when anyone who can afford to leaves for their summer homes), the streets of the Village are always crowded. The East Village and the neighbouring West Village are jam-packed with restaurants, bars, lounges, comedy clubs, small theatres and tattoo parlours. In fact, with all the places to hang out (with most of them being open until 04:00), and the various street vendors selling jewellery, hats and sunglasses, the Village can at times seem like one big street fair.

Just north of East 5th Street you will find a small Indian community so if you're after some genuine spicy food, this is where you should be headed.

If you want to burn off the calories and see some sights, East River Park, which has baseball fields, walking trails and an amphitheatre, is a great place to spend a couple of hours. Another popular activity, when the weather is good, is walking along the footpath of the Williamsburg Bridge.

If you only do one thing in...
East Village

Check out the buzzing bar scene – especially on a Friday night when the whole world seems to be out on the town.

Best for...

Eating: Sample the nostalgic, country-style menu at Prune (p.205).

Drinking: Enjoy a beer in rough, yet charming, surroundings at McSorley's Old Ale House (p.205).

Sightseeing: Simply stroll around the area to take in the bohemian atmosphere and marvel at the gothic architecture.

Shopping: St Mark's Place is home to alternative, goth and punk fashions and some excellent music stores.

Outdoor: Take a walk along the footpath of the Williamsburg bridge or spend some time in East River Park when the weather is fine.

Financial District & City Hall

It has a rich history, it's where fortunes are made and lost, and it's the site of one of the world's greatest, and most recent, tragedies. The Financial District is a fascinating area to explore.

As the oldest part of the city, the Financial District is packed with landmarks, parks, museums and famous addresses. Battery Park sits at the bottom of Manhattan Island, and Bowling Green is supposedly where Manhattan was transferred from the Native Americans to the Dutch in exchange for trinkets worth about $24. Wall Street is the traditional heart of the city's financial area, and nearby you'll find the site of the World Trade Center towers.

Battery Park
State & Whitehall St

212 267 9700
www.bpcparks.org

This 21 acre park occupies the southern tip of Manhattan, offering incredible harbour views, and doubles as the site of the original Dutch settlement. Few people are aware of the buzz beneath the park where a lot of the city's southern side infrastructure hides, including the Brooklyn-Battery tunnel, the Battery Park Underpass and the South Ferry Subway stop. In 2005, while digging beneath the park, authorities discovered the remains of a 200 year old stone wall, believed to be part of the gun batteries that once protected the city and possibly even gave the park its name. Map C 1

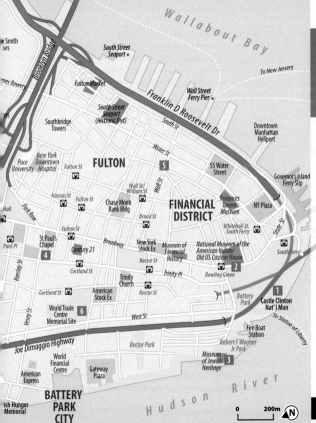

Wallabout Bay

To New Jersery

Brooklyn Bridge

Smith
ses

mes Bower

South Street
Seaport

Fulton Market

Wall Street
Ferry Pier

Franklin D Roosevelt Dr

South Street
Seaport
(Historic Dist)

Southbridge
Towers

South St

Downtown
Manhattan
Heliport

Pace
University

New York
Downtown
Hospital

Fulton St

FULTON

Water St

5

55 Water
Street

Governor's Island
Ferry Slip

Nassau St

Fulton St

Wall St/
William St

Chase Monh
Bank Bldg

Broad St

FINANCIAL
DISTRICT

Fraunces
Tavern
Museum

NY Plaza

Hall

Park Row

Fulton St

St Paul's
Chapel

Century 21

Broadway

New York
Stock Ex

Museum of
Financial
History

Whitehall St
South Ferry

National Museum of the
American Indian/
Old US Custom House

State St

Park Pl

4

Rector St

Cortland St

Trinity
Church

Trinity Pl

Bowling Green

2

South Ferry

Barclay St

Cortland St

American
Stock Ex

Rector St

Battery
Park

1

Vesey St

World Trade
Centre
Memorial Site

6

West St

Castle Clinton
Nat'l Mon

To Statue of Liberty

Joe DiMaggio Highway

Rector Park

Fire Boat
Station

Robert F Wagner
Jr Park

American
Express

World
Financial
Centre

Gateway
Plaza

Museum of
Jewish
Heritage

3

ish Hunger
Memorial

BATTERY
PARK
CITY

Hudson River

0   200m

N

C

Bowling Green and The Battery
Broadway, at Whitehall and State Streets

This is where it all began. The Dutch founded their settlement of New Amsterdam down on the southwestern tip of Manhattan, establishing a fortification on the site of what is now Battery Park. When Peter Minuit purchased the island from its native inhabitants back in 1624, legend has it that the meeting took place on the site of Bowling Green, which later became the city's first public park. Map C 2

Museum of Jewish Heritage
36 Battery Place

646 437 4200
www.mjhnyc.org

This museum tells the story of Jewish life before, during, and after the Holocaust. Educational programmes for children and adults are scheduled regularly, and activity books are available for young visitors. There is a cafe on site as well as a shop selling Judaica and educational books. Admission is $10 for adults, $7 for seniors, $5 for students, and free for children under 12. Map C 3

St Paul's Chapel (Episcopalian)
Financial District

212 233 4164

St Paul's Chapel was completed in 1766 and is Manhattan's oldest public building in continuous use. George Washington worshipped here, as did England's King William IV. After the WTC Towers collapsed in 2001 it was one of the few buildings in the vicinity to suffer no structural damage. The church became a refuge for those involved in the 9/11 aftermath, and it hosts a moving memorial display in its chapel. Map C 4

Wall Street
Financial District

Wall Street is so named because it was once the northern boundary of the colonial city, but today it is synonymous with the world's most powerful financial institutions. Step back in time at brownstone Trinity Church (74 Trinity Place, www.trinitywallstreet.org), home to one of the city's oldest parishes, founded in 1697. The New York Stock Exchange (11 Wall Street, www.nyse.com) is not open for tours, but the oft-photographed facade is always there for the gazing. Across the street, Federal Hall (26 Wall Street, 212 845 6888, www.nps.gov/feha) marks the birthplace of American government and now houses a museum. Map C 5

World Trade Center Site
Financial District

The expanse between West and Church Streets from Vesey to Liberty Streets was once occupied by the World Trade Center. All seven buildings in the complex, including the 110 storey 'Twin Towers' were destroyed on September 11, 2001. Various factors have slowed the rebuilding process, and to date only one building – 7 World Trade – has been rebuilt. For the time being, the site is a cross between a giant construction yard and a very moving tribute to those who lost their lives that day. Some of the photos taken at the time of the attacks have been enlarged and posted at the site, and there is also a fascinating timeline of how events unfolded on the day. Map C 6

Exploring

If you only do one thing in...

Financial District & City Hall

Pay your respects at Ground Zero – though largely a building site now, the photography display and timeline bring the 9/11 attacks into perspective.

Best for...

Eating: Sink a hefty burger on the waterfront deck at SouthWest NY (p.215).

Drinking: Catch up on your history at Fraunces Tavern (p.215), where George Washington and his peers used to meet.

Sightseeing: Take a sunset walk over the Brooklyn Bridge (p.125) for breathtaking views of the Manhattan skyline.

Shopping: Bag a bargain at Century 21 (p.174), where a good rummage through the racks can yield some designer finds.

Outdoor: Soak up the sun in the 21 acres of Battery Park while taking in the fantastic harbour views.

Gramercy Park & FlatironDistrict

The exclusivity of Gramercy Park and the bustle of the Flatiron District complement each other. Start at the instantly recognisable Flatiron building and head east for a lesson in contrast.

Gramercy Park, though owned by the city, is locked and accessible only to those that live in the stunning townhouses on its border. For a brief peek, visit on Gramercy Day; it is the one day a year – usually the first Saturday in May – when the gates are opened to the public. Alternatively, fork out the $500 or so that it will cost you to spend the night at the Gramercy Park Hotel (p.37) – the hotel has 12 keys to the park that are available to guests. Even if you don't manage to get the key to the door, you can still enjoy the leafy tranquillity of this area (from outside the park's fence) and mingle with lavender-rinse ladies and their Burberry-coated lapdogs.

Nearby you'll find Murray Hill, a residential area that caters to the post-collegiate, shared-apartment set. If you're hankering for a great vindaloo, this is the place – its plethora of authentic Indian restaurants has earned it the nickname 'Curry Hill'. Shoppers in search of spices should head to Kalustyan's (123 Lexington Avenue at 28th Street), a shop that also sells all matter of nuts, dried fruit, Middle Eastern-style breads, imported groceries, and some of the best home-made dips and sauces to be found in town. Get cheese, or a good cheese-based meal, at Artisanal on Park Avenue at 33rd Street

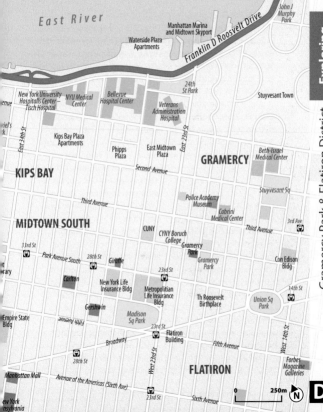

East River

Manhattan Marina
and Midtown Skyport

John J
Murphy
Park

Waterside Plaza
Apartments

Franklin D Roosevelt Drive

24th
St Park

New York University
Hospitals Center –
Tisch Hospital

NYU Medical
Center

Bellevue
Hospital Center

Stuyvesant Town

Veterans
Administration
Hospital

East 24th St

Kips Bay Plaza
Apartments

Phipps
Plaza

East Midtown
Plaza

GRAMERCY

Beth-Israel
Medical Center

East 23rd St

KIPS BAY

Second Avenue

Third Avenue

Stuyvesant Sq

MIDTOWN SOUTH

Police Academy
Museum

Cabrini
Medical Center

Third Avenue

3rd Ave

CUNY

CYNY Boruch
College

Gramercy
Park

33rd St

Park Avenue South

28th St

Giraffe

Gramercy
Park

Con Edison
Bldg

Carlton

New York Life
Insurance Bldg

23rd St

Empire State
Bldg

Gershwin

Fifth Avenue

Metropolitian
Life Insurance
Bldg

Madison
Sq Park

Th Roosevelt
Birthplace

Union Sq
Park

14th St

West 14th St

Broadway

23rd St

Flatiron
Building

Fifth Avenue

Manhattan Mall

28th St

Avenue of the Americas (Sixth Ave)

West 23rd St

FLATIRON

Forbes
Magazine
Galleries

New
York
nsylvania

23rd St

Sixth Avenue

0   250m

D

(212 725 8585), both a shop and a bistro, or for something a bit meatier, Blue Smoke (116 East 27th Street at Park Avenue) sells upscale barbecue, Sarge's Deli (548 Third Avenue at 37th Street, 212 679 0442) serves a mean pastrami sandwich which you can enjoy with a beer should you wish, and Penelope (159 Lexington Avenue at 30th Street, 212 481 3800) makes the best BBLT around – that's double bacon by the way.

Many assume that Union Square commemorates the Union's victory in the American Civil War, but it was actually named years before the war in reference to its location at the intersection of several major streets. It has long been a spot for political rallies and public events, most notably the site of America's first Labour Day celebration in 1882 and a large informal memorial after the World Trade Center attacks on September 11th, 2001. Today the park is home to the city's largest greenmarket, where local farmers, dairy producers, fishermen, and butchers sell their wares to discerning urban chefs. From late November to Christmas, the Union Square Holiday Market pops up with stalls selling all types of gifts and crafts while in summer, the park has an outdoor cafe and bar on its northern border. The park's

Privileged For A Day

Mark the first Saturday in May in your diary: this is usually Gramercy Day, when the supremely exclusive park is open to the masses. If you happen to be around on that day, you can walk into the park that is usually under lock and key – and keys are only given to those lucky enough to live in one of the grand townhouses facing the park.

equestrian statue of George Washington is a popular spot for meeting friends – or blind dates.

History fans can learn more about one of America's most beloved Presidents at the Theodore Roosevelt Birthplace (28 East 20th Street at Broadway). Music publishers and songwriters once congregated on the street nicknamed 'Tin Pan Alley,' 28th Street between Sixth Avenue and Broadway, from the 1880s to the 1930s.

Inside Madison Square, Shake Shack (212 889 6600) serves up delicious burgers and milkshakes but for fine dining in this area, head to Union Square Cafe on 16th Street (p.210), Eleven Madison Park (at 24th Street, 212 889 0905), Craft (43 East 19th Street at Broadway, 212 780 0880), or Gramercy Tavern (42 East 20th Street at Broadway, 212 477 0777), all serving American cuisine with style. For sweets, try City Bakery on 18th Street (p.212).

Large chain stores now line the stretch of lower Fifth Avenue once called 'Ladies' Mile' for its many dressmakers, but there are still a few unique shopping experiences nearby. ABC Carpet & Home (888 Broadway at 19th Street) has several floors of furniture, carpets, and home accessories, both new and antique. Fishs Eddy (889 Broadway at 19th Street) sells vintage tableware along with lines of their own design, including the popular '212' pattern depicting the New York City skyline, while for clothing bargains, Loehmann's (101 Seventh Avenue at 16th Street,) is the place to be.

BROADWAY

NO
COMMERCIAL
TRAFFIC

DEPT. OF TRAFFIC

BIKE
LANE

If you only do one thing in...
Gramercy Park & Flatiron District

Press your nose against the fence of Gramercy Park – this exclusive oasis is kept locked and only residents get a key. It is open to the public for just one day a year.

Best for:

Eating: Don't miss the chance to eat contemporary Italian-influenced fare in Union Square Cafe (p.210).

Drinking: Settle onto one of the beds and enjoy the lively vibe and Monday-Friday happy hour at Duvet Restaurant and Lounge (p.212).

Sightseeing: Admire the unusual architecture of the Flatiron Building, one of New York's most iconic landmarks.

Shopping: Head to Fish's Eddy (889 Broadway at 19th Street, 212 420 9020) to buy a dinner plate or cup decorated with the New York skyline.

Outdoor: Enjoy a cocktail and beautiful views from the rooftop bar of the Gramercy Park Hotel (p.37).

Lower East Side & Chinatown

Whether you're slurping your noodles in Chinatown, or sipping a beer on the Lower East Side, these are the areas where you can sit back, relax, and let go of that 'New York Cool'.

Lower East Side

A century ago, the Lower East Side was filled with newly arrived immigrants, many of them Jewish, all crowding into small apartments and dreaming of a better life. See the past come to life at the Tenement Museum (p.81) or one of its most historic houses of worship, the Eldridge Street Synagogue (12 Eldridge Street at Division Street). People still come to the Lower East Side in the hopes of a better life, but they are as likely to be living in a luxury loft conversion as in a tenement. Note that Third and Fourth Avenues merge to become Bowery downtown, a street that was once the site of Dutch farms (bouwerie), later a stretch of squatters' flats and homeless shelters where you'd see the 'Bowery Bums', and now home to trendy bars and a restaurant supply district.

Past and present collide in the old neighbourhood shops, many selling the best versions of Jewish speciality foods that have become iconic New York eats. Follow in the footsteps of 60 years of shoppers at Essex Street Market (120 Essex Street at Rivington Street), where a fishmonger, butcher, baker, kosher wine merchant, two cheesemongers, and several grocers supply the neighbourhood cooks. The Lower East

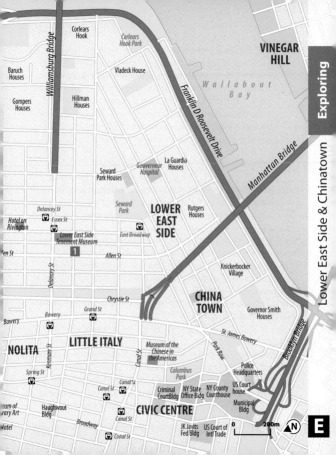

Williamsburg Bridge

Corlears Hook

Corlears Hook Park

VINEGAR HILL

Baruch Houses

Vladeck House

Wallabout Bay

Gompers Houses

Hillman Houses

Franklin D Roosevelt Drive

Manhattan Bridge

Seward Park Houses

Gouverneur Hospital

La Guardia Houses

Delancey St

Essex St

Seward Park

LOWER EAST SIDE

Rutgers Houses

Hotel on Rivington

East Broadway

Lower East Side Tenement Museum

1

Delancey St

Allen St

Knickerbocker Village

Chrystie St

CHINA TOWN

Governor Smith Houses

Bowery

Bowery

Grand St

Brooklyn Bridge

St. James Bowery

NOLITA

LITTLE ITALY

Kenmare St

Museum of the Chinese in the Americas

Park Row

Police Headquarters

Spring St

Canal St

Columbus Park

NY State Office Bldg

NY County Courthouse

US Court house

Canal St

Criminal Court Bldg

Municipal Bldg

um of rary Art

Haughwout Bldg

Canal St

CIVIC CENTRE

Broadway

Canal St

JK Javits Fed Bldg

US Court of Intl Trade

0   200m

N

E

Side bustles at night, with lots of bars and music venues in a relatively small area. The places to see new bands play are Bowery Ballroom (6 Delancey Street at Bowery, 212 533 2111), Mercury Lounge on Houston at Essex Street (p.219), and Tonic (107 Norfolk Street at Delancey Street, 212 358 7501). To be the one onstage, try punk rock karaoke night at former bodega-turned bar Arlene's Grocery on Stanton at Ludlow Street (p.218)

Have What She Had

Katz's Deli on Houston at Ludlow Street (p.217), opened in 1888, is the oldest in town – everyone should eat here at least once, if not once a month. Come hungry, and order a pastrami on rye, potato pancakes, and a Dr. Brown's Cel-Ray soda, or a traditional New York egg cream. Admire the photos of famous visitors and the memorabilia from When Harry Met Sally, the film that made the place even more famous.

Chinatown

For many visitors, Chinatown is the collection of stalls lining Canal Street between Bowery and West Broadway, half of them selling counterfeit designer handbags, sunglasses, watches, perfume, and jewellery, and the other half selling cheap souvenirs and Chinese novelties. Look beyond the $20 'Prada' purses and the plastic dragons to find a pair of the city's best shops, Pearl River Mart (477 Broadway at Broome Street) selling clothes, housewares, food and gifts, and Pearl Paint (308 Canal Street at Mercer Street) which bills itself as 'The World's Largest Discount Art Supplier.'

When hunger strikes, dumpling and noodle shops abound, as do Chinese restaurants, many of which specialise in Cantonese dishes.

Five Points

Today's Chinatown was once the site of America's most notorious slum; you can get the idea by watching Martin Scorcese's film *Gangs of New York*. Before construction of the Foley Square courthouse complex, Baxter, Worth and Park Streets intersected at five corners, forming the Five Points. Home to Irish immigrants and African-American migrants in the mid 19th century, the rough neighbourhood is credited with giving birth to tap dancing as a blend of African stepping and the Irish jig.

Lower East Side Tenement Museum   212 431 0233
90 Orchard Street   www.tenement.org

This wonderful museum consists of a set of fully furnished family apartments recreating working class immigrant life in a typical New York tenement building from 1863 to 1935. Visitors are required to choose from a selection of guided tours that deal with particular aspects of the building's history and the lives of the families who once lived there. The museum also offers 90 minute walking tours of the Lower East Side from spring through to autumn, and a variety of educational programmes year round. Admission is $15 for adults, $11 for seniors and students, and free for children under 12. Call to inquire about tours appropriate for children under five.

Map E **1**

If you only do one thing in...

Lower East Side & Chinatown

Order a pastrami on rye at Katz's Deli (p.217), and recreate Meg Ryan's classic faking scene from the movie *When Harry Met Sally*.

Best for...

Eating: Slurp up a steaming bowl of noodles or rice porridge in Chinatown, where you can be sure the taste is authentic.

Drinking: Catch up with the city's up-and-coming rockstars at Arlene's Grocery (p.218).

Sightseeing: See how the poorer half lived in the early 20th century at the Lower East Side Tenement Museum (p.81).

Shopping: The streets of Chinatown are lined with stalls where you can pick up some fascinating little trinkets, as well as – shhhhh – fake designer bags.

Outdoor: Stroll along the banks of the East River for a great peek into New York's busy waterways.

Midtown & Hells Kitchen

With a high concentration of tourist attractions, this area is always frenetic. So walk fast, talk fast, and get swept up in the energy of the multicultural crowd.

There is lots to see and do in this area. Outdoor spaces of note include Times Square (42nd to 48th Streets between Broadway and Eighth Avenue) and Bryant Park, home of the New York Public Library (42nd Street and Fifth Avenue). New York's two most beloved skyscrapers are here; the Empire State Building (34th Street and Fifth Avenue) and the Chrysler Building (42nd Street and Lexington Avenue) and you'll also find St Patrick's Cathedral (Fifth Avenue and 50th Street) and Central Synagogue (East 55th Street at Lexington Avenue) two of the most impressive houses of worship in the city.

Tours of the United Nations (First Avenue between 42nd and 48th Streets) can be fun, but the traffic when the General Assembly is in session is definitely not. Do not leave town without taking in a concert at Carnegie Hall (West 57th Street at Seventh Avenue). If culture is your thing, MoMA (the Museum of Modern Art, p.88) lives up to its hype, and both the American Folk Art Museum (p.87) and the Museum of Television and Radio (p.89) are worth a visit. The world's largest department store, Macy's at Herald Square (p.176), anchors the bustling shopping corridor along 34th Street between Fifth and Ninth Avenues.

Midtown & Hells Kitchen

East River

Tunnel

Franklin D Roosevelt Drive

Waterside Plaza Apartments

First Avenue

United Nations Headquarters

United Nations Plaza

NYU Medical Center

Bellevue Hospital Center

Manhattan Arts and Antique Center

Chile

Israel

New Zealand

East 34th St

Second Avenue

United Kingdom

East 42nd St

Switzerland

Australia

Third Avenue

Hong Kong

Ireland

Grand Hyatt

Park Avenue

Westvaco Bldg
Waldorf=Astoria

33rd St

Park Avenue South

Giraffe

Germany

New York Palace

270 Park

Grand Central Terminal

Mexico

St Regis

Roosevelt

Pierpont Morgan Library

Canada

Museum of Modern Art

St Patrick's Cathedral

4

5th Ave

Gershwin

Madison Sq Park

1 5

Saks Fifth Avenue

New York Public Library

Lord & Taylor

Fifth Avenue

Warwick

Rockefeller Plaza

GE Bldg

The Algonquin

2

Empire State Bldg

3

Hilton & Town Hall

Bryant Park

Broadway

Sheraton New York

Casablanca

Manhattan Mall

Avenue of the Americas (Sixth Ave)

Michelangelo

Broadway

49th St

Times Square

Macy's

28th St

Marriott Marquis

6

Hilton Times Square

Navarre Bldg

Madison Square Garden

Seventh Avenue

Chelsea

50th St

42nd St

Belvedere

Eighth Avenue

34th St
Penn Station

New York Penn Station

23rd St

St Clare's Hospital

HELLS KITCHEN

West 42nd St

Bus Terminal

Port Authority

Ninth Avenue

General Post Office

Skyline

West 34th St

Chelsea Park

Tenth Avenue

Travel Inn

CHELSEA

West 27th St

Vitt Park

Twelveth Avenue

Joe Dimaggio Highway

China

Tunnel

JK Javits Exhibition and Convention Center of New York

30th Street Terminal

Eleventh Avenue

Hudson River Park

Joe Dimaggio Highway

300m

N

F

Hell's Kitchen

The gritty streets of Hell's Kitchen, a subsection of Midtown that runs from the Hudson River to Ninth Avenue in the 40s and 50s, were allegedly the inspiration for the rough neighbourhood depicted in the musical *West Side Story*. Gentrification has brought housing prices up, but plenty of areas still look run down, especially around the Port Authority Bus Terminal (42nd Street and Eighth Avenue). Rudy's (Ninth Avenue at 44th Street) will provide a free hot dog with every pint of beer purchased, but Hallo Berlin (10th Avenue at 45th Street, 212 977 1944) does a much better job with its sausages. Daisy May's BBQ USA (11th Avenue at 46th Street, 212 977 1500) makes some great slow-cooked pork – you might spot some of their carts on the city streets. Tony Luke's (576 Ninth Avenue at 42nd Street, 212 967 3055) sells the finest cheesesteak sandwich this side of Philadelphia while Don't Tell Mama (343 West 46th Street at Eighth Avenue, 212 757 0788) is a classic piano bar and a New York institution so you'll feel like a well-fed local in no time.

Best Views

Visiting Depression-era gem Rockefeller Center (48th to 51st Street between Fifth and Seventh Avenues) just got better with the new and improved three observation decks at the Top of the Rock (www.topoftherocknyc.com) on the 70th floor; its Radio City Music Hall, America's largest indoor theatre, is the home of the world's most popular Christmas show, starring the high-kicking Rockettes.

American Folk Art Museum

212 265 1040
45 W 53rd Street   www.folkartmuseum.org

This museum opens a window onto folk culture from the past 300 years. Adults and children alike enjoy well-curated displays of homespun drawings, paintings, sculptures, textiles, and photographs by self-taught artists from all parts of the country. The hand-made textile collection is a highlight, including the 9/11 National Tribute Quilt. The museum sponsors two popular annual events in January: The American Antiques Show and Outsider Art Week (in conjunction with the Outsider Art Fair). Tours, craft workshops, classes for children and adults, lectures, and symposia are held on an ongoing basis. Admission is $9 for adults, $7 for seniors and students, and free for children under 12. Map F **1**

Bryant Park

212 768 4242
Fifth & Sixth Ave 40th – 42nd St   www.bryantpark.org

Seeped in history, conflict and controversy, Bryant Park is a slice of New York unto itself. First designated as a public space in 1686, George Washington and his troops marched across it retreating from the Battle of Long Island in 1776. From 1823 to 1840, the Park was better known as a potter's field until the bodies were finally moved, making way for the park proper in 1847. During the American Civil War the area was used for military drills and then became the gruesome site of the New York Draft Riots in 1863. Now calmer, Bryant Park offers visitors a large sitting area, free wireless internet, and a famous outdoor movie series in summer. Map F **2**

Empire State Building

Fifth Avenue and 34th Street   www.esbnyc.com

The tallest building in the world when it opened in 1931, the 1,454 foot tall Empire State Building once again became the city's top skyscraper after the destruction of the World Trade Center. The view from the observation deck stretches for 80 miles on a clear day and is well worth the price of admission. The viewing deck is open daily from 08:00 to midnight, although at certain times of the year hours are extended to 02:00. A visit to the 86th floor viewing deck costs $18 for adults, $16 for teens, and $12 for kids. Kids under 5 and military personnel in uniform go up for free. You can get a headset that gives you an audio tour for an extra $7. Access to the viewing deck on the 102nd floor costs an additional $15.

Map F **3**

Museum of Modern Art

11 W 53rd Street

212 708 9400
www.moma.org

MoMA began with just nine paintings back in 1929 and today holds over 150,000 works of art, 22,000 films, and a library of more than 300,000 volumes. One of the world's great modern art museums, it moved into a very modish new building designed by Yoshio Taniguchi in 2004, allowing the curators to display more of the permanent collection and creating more space for educational programming. Highlights from MoMA's permanent collection of painting and sculpture reside on the fourth and fifth floors, including work by Monet, Van Gogh, Picasso, Matisse, Pollack, Warhol and Cezanne, but the photography and drawing exhibits on the third floor are also recommended. Admission is $20 for adults, $16 for seniors, $12 for students, and free for children under 16. Map F 4

Museum of Television and Radio

212 621 6800
25 W 52nd Street
www.mtr.org

The name says it all. If it went out over the airwaves, and was worth watching or hearing, it is probably archived here and available for viewing (or listening) by appointment. It's a great way to catch rare episodes of classic programmes. Visitors simply drop in for public airings or enjoy their selections in a private console. One tip: when watching early television shows, the commercial breaks are often as much fun as the shows themselves! Admission is $10 for adults, $8 for seniors and students, and $5 for children under 14. Map F 5

Times Square

42nd to 48th Streets, btn Broadway & 8th Ave

Times Square, named for its famous tenant, The *New York Times*, runs from 42nd Street to 48th Streets between Broadway and Eighth Avenue and its centre is, in fact, a triangle. One of the city's most recognisable streetscapes, its by-ways are packed with pedestrians nearly every day of the year. It's one of New York's tourism meccas, so apart from being busy nearly all the time, it's also where you'll find touristy hangouts like the Bubba Gump Shrimp Company! Every New Year's Eve, the televised celebrations are attended by hundreds of thousands of revellers. Map F 6

If you only do one thing in...
Midtown & Hells Kitchen

Go to the Top of the Rock at the Rockefeller Center for panoramic views of the city, including Central Park.

Best for...

Eating: Quaff the freshest raw oysters at the Grand Central Oyster Bar (p.224), amid the bustling vibe of Grand Central Station.

Drinking: Claim your space on a velvet couch or boogie to mainstream hits at the Grand (p.225).

Sightseeing: Experience the view from the top of the Empire State Building (p.88). Long queues give you the time to admire the impressive art deco interior.

Shopping: It's a toss-up between the grandeur of Fifth Avenue (p.166) and Macy's, the city's largest department store (p.176).

Outdoor: Enjoy an alfresco cocktail at AVA Lounge (p.224). The views are stunning.

Noho, Nolita & Little Italy

Spaghetti and shopping combine to make these areas delightful. Feast on a plate of heavenly pasta before exploring Nolita's quirky range of shops and musing through Noho's galleries.

Nolita, an abbreviation for 'North of Little Italy,' is best known as a boutique shopping destination; a sort of low-key extension of Soho. There are many small shops along Mulberry, Mott, Prince and Elizabeth Streets, the majority selling women's clothing and accessories. Sigerson Morrison (28 Prince Street at Mott Street) and Otto Tootsi Plohound (273 Lafayette Street at Prince Street) are paradise for shoe fanatics while Francophiles might try Pylones (69 Spring Street at Lafayette Street) for colourful toys, accessories, and housewares from Paris. Everyone should head to Lunettes et Chocolat (25 Prince Street at Mott Street) for an unlikely mix of eyewear and candies. Just across the street from the 1815 landmark Old St Patrick's Church (260 Mulberry Street at Prince Street) is Café Gitane on Mott Street (p.228), a great place for coffee, while the focus is on after-dinner treats at innovative wine and dessert bar Room 4 Dessert (17 Cleveland Place at Kenmare Street).

If you're on the lookout for some gorgeous vintage clothing pieces, Nolita is a great area. Resurrection (217 Mott Street, 212 625 1374) stocks some beautiful pieces dating back to the 60s.

on Sq North

Astor Pl

Marks Pl

on Square Park

Waverly Pl

Second Avenue

NOHO

Greene St

Mercer St

East 5th St

Merchant's House
Museum

NY University

East 4th St

First Avenue

Thompson St

Broadway

East 3rd St

Washington
Square Village

Bleecker St

East 2nd St

Mercer St

University Plaza

West Houston St

East 1st St

Broadway Lafayette

Lafayette St

Museum of African Art

East Houston St

2nd Ave

New Museum of
Contemporary Art

Stanton St

Eldridge St

Mercer Hotel

Prince St

Allen St

enheim
um SoHo

Prince St

Greene St

Mercer St

Cosby St

NOLITA

Rivington St

Bowery

Forsyth St

HO

Spring St

Spring St

Broome St

Kenmare St

Delancey St

Haughwout
Bldg

Mulberry St

Bowery

Sarah
Roosevelt Park

Mott St

Lafayette St

Centre St

Elizabeth St

Broome St

Grand St

Baxter St

Mercer St

Broadway

Grand St

Grand St

Canal St

Chrystie St

Eldridge St

Allen St

Canal St

Hester St

LITTLE ITALY

r St

Canal St

Hester St

0   100m   N

At Cat Fish Greetings on Mulberry Street, you can pick up a handmade card for any occasion, as well as special infant T-shirts with a pumpkin or cupcake emblazoned across them for just $22.

Little Italy was once a proper neighbourhood, but it is now little more than the strip of shops and restaurants on Mulberry Street. The Bronx's Arthur Avenue or Brooklyn's Bensonhurst and Bay Ridge neighbourhoods are much better places to find Italian-American food, but a few of the tourist spots here are better than average. Da Nico (164 Mulberry Street at Grand Street, 212 343 1212) is a great restaurant for groups, Ferrara Pasticceria (108 Mulberry Street at Canal Street) is good for coffee and a pastry on the go, and Di Palo Fine Italian Foods (206 Grand Street at Mott Street) will happily supply you with imported goodies.

Some restaurants of note in Little Italy include the famous Umberto's Clam House (www.umbertosclamhouse.com), and Il Cortile (212 226 6060). And the neighbourhood still celebrates the Feast of San Gennaro for 11 days each

San Gennaro

The best time, or the worst according to some, to visit Little Italy is during San Gennaro. This street festival has been held in honour of the patron saint of Sicily annually since 1927, and it has got bigger every year. For 10 days in September, over a million people pack themselves into Mulberry Street to eat, drink, be merry, and buy schlocky souvenirs. It is something to see, but the crowds easily become overwhelming.

September. The entire street closes to vehicular traffic and pedestrians are free to stroll from one food vendor to another.

Find out more about Little Italy on the area's official website: www.littleitalynyc.com. It has information on restaurants, shopping and events, and you can even print out discount coupons to redeem at businesses in the area. Tucked between Greenwich Village and the East Village, the architecturally unique Noho (North of Houston) offers a wealth of off-centre bars and cafés intertwined with hip clothing boutiques and performance spaces. Other Music (15 East 4th Street) is considered one of the top independent music retailers in the country while Joe's Pub and the Public Theater (425 Lafayette Street) provide hip audiences with nightly music and theatre performances. If fitting in with the local hipsters is a priority, outfit yourself with shoes from David Z (620 Broadway) and accessories from Bond 07 (7 Bond Street). Then head out to enjoy rare vodkas in the Temple Bar (332 Lafayette Street; marked by an Iguana), stylish sushi from Bond Street (6 Bond Street), or cheap Cajun cuisine at Great Jones Café (54 Great Jones Street).

Take a fragrant souvenir home with you: Bond No. 9 (Broadway & Lafayette, 212 228 1732) sells perfumes that capture the essence of NYC. Take home a bottle of Chinatown, Chelsea Flowers, Wall Street or Broadway Nite to remind you of the city that never sleeps, or create your own perfume in store.

Even though this is one of the smallest areas in Manhattan, you could definitely spend at least a day exploring Nolita, Noho and Little Italy.

If you only do one thing in...
Noho, Nolita & Little Italy

Soak up the Italian atmosphere in Little Italy, where you can sample authentic food treats from the many Italian restaurants, bakeries and delis.

Best for...
Eating: Escape to the countryside at Il Buco (p.227), possibly the most rustic restaurant in Manhattan.

Drinking: If you think all tequilas are equal, head to La Esquina (p.229), where you'll get an education in the various incarnations of the strong stuff.

Sightseeing: Find your culture off the beaten track in Noho, which has several acclaimed art galleries.

Shopping: Nolita's boutiques range from the quirky to the trendy, and this is one of the best areas in which to shop for vintage clothing.

Outdoor: Grab a slice of the best from Lombardi's pizzeria (p.228) and eat it while walking for true New York street cred.

Tribeca & Soho

Two of the hottest neighbourhoods in the city compete for your attention side by side. Spend a day here for access to the artistic culture and nightlife that New York is famous for.

Tribeca is an abbreviation for 'Triangle Below Canal,' a neighbourhood bounded by the river and Broadway. Until just a few decades ago it was an unremarkable industrial district, but now luxury loft conversions abound, as do upmarket restaurants and bars. One of the best is Bouley on West Broadway at Duane Street (p.242), with an honourable mention for Danube (30 Hudson Street at Duane Street, 212 791 3771) which is owned by the same chef. Capsouto Freres (451 Washington Street at Watts Street, 212 966 4900) is a classic French bistro, while City Hall (131 Duane Street at Church Street, 212 227 7777) does it American style with a New York theme. If you have little ones in the Big Apple then head to Bubby's on Hudson Street at North Moore Street (p.240) which is ideal for children, with a menu of American comfort food appealing to all ages and plenty of crayons on the table for entertainment.

For a quick bite on the go, try a veggie combo at Pakistan Tea House (176 Church Street at Reade Street, 212 240 9800), a gourmet sandwich at 'Wichcraft (397 Greenwich Street and Beach Street, www.wichcraftnyc.com), or a Cubano at Columbine (229 West Broadway at White Street, 212 965

Vandam St

Spring Street
Terminal

Spring St

Spring St

Spring St

SOHO

Dominic St

60 Thompson

Thompson St

Hudson St

Broome St

Broome St

Wooster St

Varick St

W Broadway

Grand St

Canal St

Watts St

Canal St

Canal St

SoHo Grand

Desbrosses St

Washington St

Greenwich St

Vestry St

St Johns Ln

Laight St

Hudson Square

Lispenard St

NY Telephone Bldg

Walker St

Hubert St

Ericsson St

Sixth Ave

W Broadway

White St

Beach St

Varick St

Franklin St

Hudson St

N Moore St

Franklin St

Franklin St

Leonard St

Harrison St

Franklin St

Joe Dimaggio Highway

West St

Jay St

Western Union Bldg

Worth St

CUNY Borough of
Manhattan College

Greenwich St

AT&T Bldg

Thomas St

Duane St

Washington
Market Park

...son A
...er Park

Chambers St

Chambers St

Reade St

N End Ave

Chambers St

Chambers St

Warren St

Chambers St

100m

N

H

TRIBECA

0909). Drinks are cosy at bar and bistro Lucky Strike (59 Grand Street at West Broadway, 212 941 0772), see a scene at the bar inside the Soho Grand Hotel on West Broadway at Canal Street (p.40), and there are no frills at Nancy Whisky Pub on Lispenard Street at West Broadway (212 226 9943).

Soho is the area 'South of Houston,' north of Canal Street, and between Crosby Street and West Broadway. Remember that it's pronounced HOWS-ton, never HEWS-ton. The dozens of handsome cast iron buildings were first industrial sites, then they became artists' lofts, and now they have become luxury lofts. You can't throw a credit card without hitting a shop in Soho, and it's possible to purchase anything from $5 vintage dresses to $500,000 couture gowns.

The Guggenheim SoHo, located on Broadway and Prince, is a tiny segment of the mighty Guggenheim. It is open from 11:00 to 18:00 every day except for Tuesdays and Wednesdays, when it is closed. Admission is free.

Bloomingdale's (504 Broadway at Broome Street) downtown branch is in the midst of a packed shopping corridor on Broadway, a run of commercial storefronts that actually begins near Union Square and continues past Canal Street. Clothes and shoes dominate, but there are other gems to be found. Kate's Paperie (561 Broadway at Prince Street) is great for stationery, gift-wrap, and greeting cards. Local gourmands pay up for the fine foods at Dean & Deluca on Broadway at Prince Street (p.250), and get bottles from New York State's often surprising good vineyards at Vintage New York on Broome Street at Wooster Street (212 226 9463). Everything is good at Jacques Torres Chocolate (350

Hudson Street at Charleton Street, www.mrchocolate.com), but the hot chocolate is to die for. Moss (146 Greene Street at Prince Street) has housewares that approach fine art, while Evolution's (130 Spring Street at Mercer Street) selection of taxidermy, fossils, rocks, and shells would look at home in the Museum of Natural History.

Everything is fresh from the sea at Aquagrill (210 Spring Street at Sullivan Street, 212 274 0505), and the bar is a great place to get cocktails and oysters. Balthazar on Spring Street (p.242) has been a trendy spot for years, but the food also lives up to its hype and be sure to order the breadbasket at brunch, or stock the pantry with a box to go from Balthazar Bakery next door. For drinks, Fanelli's (94 Prince Street at Mercer Street, 212 226 9412) is a cafe and bar with old-fashioned appeal, while Milady's bar (160 Prince Street at Thompson Street, 212 226 9340) draws a younger crowd from nearby NYU.

Soho Art Galleries

Soho, once the place to shop for art, is now just an all-around shopping district. Between all the clothing boutiques and housewares shops, there are still several dozen galleries, mainly along Broadway, Prince, and Wooster Streets. Good bets in Soho and the immediate area include Bond Gallery (5 Rivington Street), Rivington Arms (102 Rivington Street), Louis K Meisel (141 Prince Street), Deitch Projects (18 Wooster Street) and Wooster Arts Space (147 Wooster Street). Visit www.artseensoho.com for show listings and a printable map of area galleries.

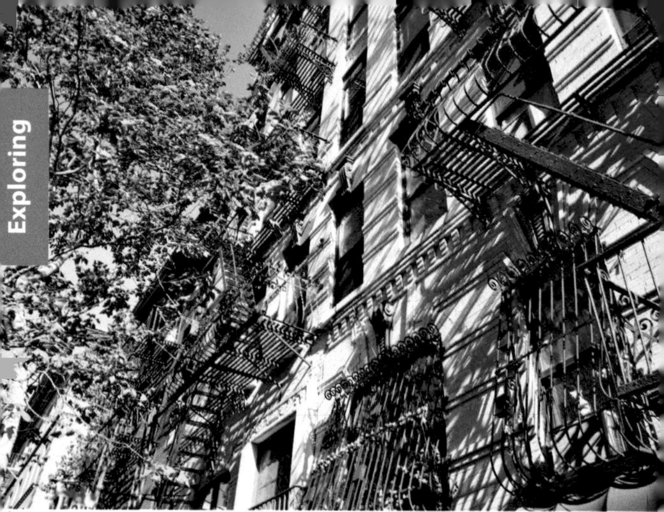

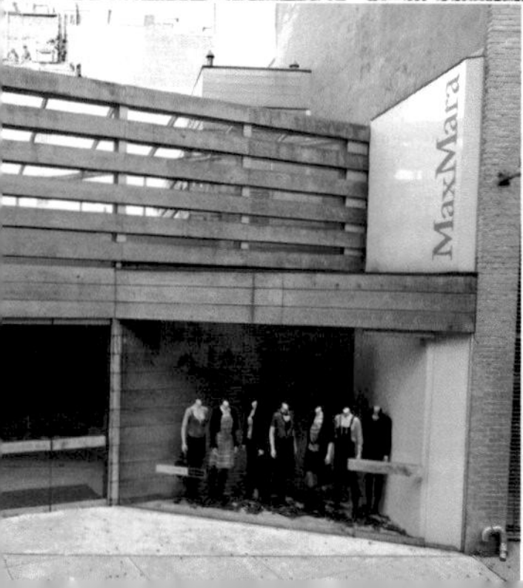
MaxMara

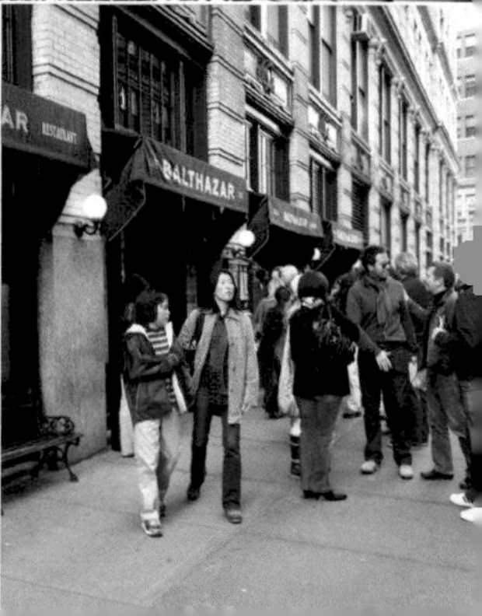
BALTHAZAR

If you only do one thing in...
Tribeca & Soho

Treat yourself to a meal in Bouley (p.242), regularly rated as New York's finest restaurant.

Best for...

Eating: There is a concentration of amazing restaurants in this area, so if your budget doesn't stretch to Bouley, theres a long list of alternatives.

Drinking: Nurture your sophisticated side at Brandy Library Lounge (p.244).

Sightseeing: There are many galleries and museums in the area, including a branch of the Guggenheim.

Shopping: Load up your credit card in preparation, because Soho is one of the best shopping areas in the city.

Outdoor: Just wander up or down Broadway between Canal and Houston Streets for a unique mix of shops and eateries that personify the area.

Upper East Side & Central Park

Take the time to explore 'New York's back yard' – Central Park is a refreshing pocket of greenery amid the concrete chaos. It is flanked to the east by some of the most expensive real estate in the world – the Upper East Side.

The Upper East Side is home to many of the wealthiest New Yorkers. When people speak of having 'the right address' they mean right here on Fifth and Park Avenues. Central Park is an oasis of greenery in the middle of the city, while over on the river, Carl Schurz Park is the preferred recreation spot for the east side of the neighbourhood, and the home of the mayor's official residence, Gracie Mansion. For great views, hop on the aerial tram to Roosevelt Island at 59th Street and walk its waterfront promenade and park.

This area is where you'll find Museum Mile, with the Met (p.108), the Whitney (p.109), the Guggenheim (p.107), the Neue Galerie (p.109), the Museum of the City of New York (p.108), the Cooper-Hewitt (p.106), the Jewish Museum (p.107), the Asia Society (725 Park Avenue at 71st Street), and the Frick Collection (1 East 70th Street at Fifth Avenue) all within walking distance. As for shopping, every designer worth their threads has a shop on Madison or Fifth Avenues, keeping the neighbourhood awash in posh labels and stylish couture.

Central Park

60th St – 110th St

212 310 6600
www.centralparknyc.org

The most visited park in the United States, the 834 acres is an oasis in the NYC urban jungle and a real gem in the city's historical crown. Drawing some 25 million visitors each year, 'New York's backyard' is still the perfect place to escape the madding crowd. You can skate on Wollman Rink (p.149) in winter, and play a few innings at Heckscher Ballfields in the lazy summer months. Map J **1**

Central Park Wildlife Center & Tisch Children's Zoo

5th Ave & East 64th St

212 439 6500
www.nyzoosandaquarium.com

Central Park's small zoo is a popular family destination, welcoming about a million visitors each year. The Wildlife Center's most prominent residents are its sea lions, penguins, and polar bear, while the Children's Zoo focuses on animals for petting. Open year round, daily. Admission is $8 for adults, $4 for seniors, $3 for children 3-12, and free for children under 3. Map J **2**

Cooper-Hewitt National Design Museum

2 E 91st St

212 849 8400
www.ndm.si.edu

America's only design museum holds 250,000 objects, including industrial products, home furnishings, textiles, and graphic designs from around the world. The museum has daily tours and a number of educational programmes for children and adults are held weekly. The museum's Summer

Sessions, held every Friday from 18:00 to 21:00 from June until September, are also wildly popular. Different DJs play in the gorgeous outdoor space behind the museum, and food and drink is served. Map J **3**

Guggenheim Museum

212 423 3500

1071 Fifth Ave   www.guggenheim.org

The Guggenheim's Frank Lloyd Wright building is an attraction in itself, sometimes more interesting than the art inside. Founded to showcase modern paintings, the museum now focuses on large temporary exhibitions of art from ancient to modern, architecture, and design. There is a museum cafe on site, as well as a gift shop. Tours are given regularly and audio tours are available at all times. Admission is $18 for adults, $15 for seniors and students, and free for children under 12. Map J **4**

Jewish Museum

212 423 3200

1109 Fifth Ave   www.thejewishmuseum.org

This museum displays a collection of art, design, and religious objects created by Jewish artists from all parts of the world, from antiquity to the present. Special events and educational programmes are plentiful, especially around the time of Jewish holidays, and tours are conducted regularly. Café Weissman (212 423 3307) serves creative glatt kosher meals on the museum's lower level. The museum has two gift shops. Admission is $12 for adults, $10 for seniors, $7.50 for students, and free for children under 12. Map J **5**

The Metropolitan Museum of Art 212 535 7710
1000 Fifth Ave www.metmuseum.org

The Met is one of the world's great museums; an art history textbook come to life in Central Park, with a collection of over two million pieces spanning 5,000 years of human history – all viewed by more than five million visitors each year. The permanent collection includes vast holdings of American and European art, plus galleries devoted to art and objects from Asia, Africa, Oceania, Ancient Greece and Rome, Ancient Egypt, and the Islamic world. Art lovers could easily spend days exploring every gallery, but it is possible to hit all the highlights in about three to four hours. Both general and exhibition-specific tours are conducted several times daily. Admission is $20 for adults, $10 for students and seniors, and free for children under 12. Map J **6**

The Museum of the City of New York 212 534 1672
1220 Fifth Ave www.mcny.org

This museum cares about all things New York; its 450 plus years of history, current events, and the shape the city might take in the future. Exhibitions cover all aspects of city life, with something for everyone; from children's toys, domestic interiors, and restaurant menus to professional sports, transit systems, and economic trends. It would take about three or four hours to see it all, but a quick spin is possible in two. The museum is especially kid-friendly and even hosts birthday parties on site and family events on a regular basis. Admission is $9 for adults, $5 for seniors and students, and free for children under 12.

Neue Galerie Museum for German and Austrian Art

212 628 6200

1048 Fifth Ave

www.neuegalerie.org

The Neue Galerie, housed in an elegant 1914 Carrere and Hastings-designed building, focuses on early 20th-century art and design from Germany and Austria. Highlights from the permanent collection include work by Gustav Klimt, Egon Schiele, Paul Klee, Vasily Kandinsky, Marcel Breuer, and Mies van der Rohe. The museum's upscale restaurant, Café Sabarksy (212 352 2300), serves authentic Viennese cuisine, and the Design Shop sells high quality reproductions of objects found in the permanent collection. Admission is $15 for adults and $10 for seniors and students. Children under 12 are not admitted. Map J 7

Whitney Museum of American Art

212 570 3676

945 Madison Ave

www.whitney.org

The Whitney holds one of the world's largest collections of American art created from 1900 to the present, with over 12,000 pieces in total, only 1% of which is on display at any given time. Highlights from the permanent collection include work by Edward Hopper, Georgia O'Keeffe, Alexander Calder, Willem de Kooning, and Jasper Johns. Curators keep the collection fresh and up to date by acquiring new work from artists shown at the Whitney Biennial, a survey of everything of note in the contemporary American art scene. Admission is $15 for adults, $10 for seniors and students, and free for children under 12. Map J 8

Americans in Paris
1860–1900

If you only do one thing in...
Upper East Side & Central Park

Spend as much time as you can in Central Park, where you can ice skate in winter or sunbathe in summer, and enjoy some fascinating people watching throughout the year.

Best for...

Eating: Enjoy a refined, traditional afternoon tea in The Rotunda at The Pierre (p.233).

Drinking: Eschew the Upper East Side snobbery by downing a beer at unpretentious Brother Jimmy's (p.233).

Sightseeing: Enjoy an afternoon in the Metropolitan Museum of Art (p.108), one of the world's best museums.

Shopping: Two of the greatest department stores – Barneys (p.170) and Bloomingdales (p.172) are in this area.

Outdoor: It's got to be Central Park, possibly the most famous park in the world!

Upper West Side

It's a posh area with a neighbourhood feel, easy access to Central Park, a collection of several historical and cultural institutions, and some of the city's best restaurants.

The Upper West Side is the highest-density residential area in the entire country, so this residential neighbourhood is filled with families and the everyday businesses that serve them. No surprise that its landmarks are historic co-op buildings: on Central Park West, the Majestic (at 71st Street), the Dakota (at 72nd Street), and the San Remo (at 74th Street); on Broadway: the Dorilton (at 71st Street) and the Ansonia (at 73rd Street).

Central Park is very much the neighbourhood's backyard but Riverside Park, from 59th Street all the way to 158th Street, gives it a run for its money, especially for the biking and jogging set. Paths are wide and clean, and the view of the Hudson River and the New Jersey Palisades beyond is stunning. From spring until autumn, the cafe at the 79th Street Boat Basin inside the park is a great place for drinks and dinner. Find the answer to the old joke 'Who's buried in Grant's Tomb?' in the upper part of the park, where the former president's grave is a national monument.

With more than a dozen arts organisations including the Metropolitan Opera, the New York City Ballet, and the New York Philharmonic in residence at the complex, there is always something going on at Lincoln Center (Broadway from 62nd

96th St

West 96th St

96th St

North Meadow

Thalia
Theatre

All Saints
Church

South Meadow

Joane of Arc Statue

Claremont
Riding Academy

Jacqueline Kennedy
Onassis Reservoir

Soldiers and
Sailors Monument

West End Avenue

Central Park West

Manhattan School
of Arts and Sciences

86th St

86th St

**UPPER WEST
SIDE**

**Central
Park**

Mt Tom Edgar
Allan Poe's Perch

Children's
Museum of
Manhattan

The Great Lawn

Riverside Dr

Hayden
Planetarium

81st St

79th St

West 79th St

American Museum
of Natural History

Turtle Pond

Amsterdam Avenue

Shakespeare Garden

NY Historical
Society

Broadway

Columbus Avenue

The Lake

72nd St

Dakota

72nd St.

Statue of H Ch
Andersen

Strawberry Fields

Hudson River

The Sheep Meadow

West End Avenue

66th St
Lincoln Ctr

East Green

Watter reade
Theatre

**LINCOLN
SQUARE**

Metropolitian
Opera

Avery
Fisher
Hall

Henry Hudson Parkway

Fordham
University

Wollman Skating
Rink

Gulf &
Western

Playground

250m

N

CUNY John
Jay College

Roosevelt
Hospital

59th St
Columbus Cir

Columbus Centre

Columbus
Circle

Central Park South

The
Pond

West 57th St

K

to 65th Streets). The nearby Beacon Theatre (2124 Broadway at 74th Street) is also a great concert and event venue. Visit dinosaurs at the American Museum of Natural History, learn about America's oldest Jewish community at the 1654 Society (8 West 70th Street at Central Park West), and look into the city's past at the New York Historical Society (2 West 77th Street at Central Park West). Further uptown, the enormous and hauntingly beautiful Cathedral of Saint John the Divine (Amsterdam Avenue at 112th Street) is a must-see, and Riverside Church (Riverside Drive and 122nd Street) is worth a stop when in the area. Columbia University (between 114th and 120th Streets and Broadway and Amsterdam Avenues) is New York's entry in the Ivy League, while picturesque City College (138th Street and Convent Avenue) in nearby western Harlem is a public university with a storied past.

The main shopping corridors here are Amsterdam Avenue and Broadway. The two best-known shops on the Upper West Side are supermarkets: Zabar's (2245 Broadway at 80th Street) and Fairway (2127 Broadway at 74th Street); the former is famous for its lox and Jewish baked goods, and the latter has a cafe upstairs that serves a great brunch. Gracious Home (1992 Broadway at 67th Street) has housewares galore, and Labyrinth Books (536 West 112th Street at Amsterdam Avenue) will keep the shelves stocked. For one of Manhattan's few proper mall experiences, visit the swanky new Time Warner Center (p170).

Two of the city's best restaurants are right on Columbus Circle: Jean Georges at 1 Central Park West (p.235) and Per Se inside the Time Warner Center, both with three Michelin stars.

The area is known for its brunch offerings, where patrons are known to wait upwards of an hour for the first meal of the day. Barney Greengrass (541 Amsterdam Avenue at 86th Street, 212 724 4707) is the granddaddy of them all, but nearby Popover Café (551 Amsterdam Avenue at 87th Street, 212 595 8555) is not too shabby either, or skip all the fuss, get a bag of the best at H&H Bagels (2239 Broadway at 80th Street). For a classic New York hot dog head to Gray's Papaya at 71st and Broadway.

American Museum of Natural History 212 769 5100
Central Park West and 79th St   www.amnh.org

A world of scientific discovery awaits you within this palatial 1877 building. Visitors of all ages come for the displays of taxidermy animals, preserved plants, and, of course, dinosaur skeletons and fossils. The life-size whale in the Hall of Ocean Life has long been a crowd favourite, and a recent renovation has left the gallery better than ever. The collections of artefacts from 'primitive' cultures are extensive and colourful, though many have a whiff of being quaintly outdated. The Rose Center's space exhibits are equipped with the latest technology, and the Hayden Planetarium doubles as an IMAX theatre when it's not seeing stars. Seeing all that AMNH has to offer can easily fill a day, but the highlights can be toured in three hours. There are several places to eat in the museum, including a foodcourt, cafe, and juice bar. The admission suggested is $14 for adults, $10.50 for students and seniors, and $8 for children, plus fees for special exhibitions. Map K 1

If you only do one thing in...
Upper West Side

Catch some live jazz at the Lincoln Center (Broadway from 62nd to 65th Streets).

Best for...
Eating: Jean Georges (p.235), in the Trump International Hotel, continues to impress discerning diners year after year.

Drinking: Romance the one you love (or the one you're with) over a good glass of burgundy at Shalel Lounge (p.236).

Sightseeing: Take a journey of scientific discovery at the American Museum of Natural History (p.115).

Shopping: Amsterdam Avenue and Broadway are corridors of prime shopping.

Outdoor: Pay tribute to the too-short life of John Lennon at Strawberry Fields in Central Park. Yoko Ono still visits from time to time to remember the great man and meet the fans.

West Village

West Village streets are always crowded with people enjoying the many restaurants, bars, lounges, comedy clubs and theatres – explore the village and enjoy the street fair atmosphere.

The street grid that covers most of Manhattan disappears in the West Village, but it's a beautiful place to get lost. Everything here is on a smaller, more humane scale than in other city neighbourhoods. Think of Hudson River Park's manageable stretch of bike path, the many narrow, tree-lined streets, rows of stately brownstones, tiny boutiques, and cosy restaurants. Everything is small, except property prices. This famously bohemian neighbourhood has gone upscale in recent years, but there is still plenty of old-fashioned charm to be found. Keep an eye on the houses while strolling by, as plaques mark the facades of historic homes that once belonged to the likes of Theodore Dreiser, Willa Cather and EE Cummings.

New York University keeps a constant flow of young people in the area, for better or worse, with Washington Square Park serving as its unofficial quad. Check out one of the city's loveliest streets, Washington Mews, just a half block north of Washington Square North. The Lucille Lortel Theatre (121 Christopher Street at Bedford Street) has been around since 1955 under different names, always a respected Off-Broadway house. Foot-tapping culture vultures need to visit

Mercer St

Museum of African Art

New Museueum of
Contemporary Art

Prince St

Greene St

NY University

University Plaza

**GREENWICH
VILLAGE**

Washington
Square Village

Mercer

West 11th St

Fifth Avenue

Washington Sq North

Bleecker St

West Houston St

Guggenheim
Museum SoHo

1

Washington
Square
Park

Washington Sq South

Thompson St

Leo Castelli
Gallery

West 9th St

Judson
Memorial
Church

Sullivan St

West 10th St

West 8th St

MacDougal St

Prince St

West 4th St

Sixth Avenue

West 3rd St

W 4th St

Father Demo
Square

Jefferson
Market
Library

Cornelia St

Downing St

Vandam St

Waverly Pl

Jones St

Bleecker St

Carmine St

Kings St

Christopher St
Sheridan Sq

Barrow St

Leroy St

Houston St

Varick St

Seventh Avenue

Perry St

St John
Church

Grove St

Bedford St

Morton St

Hudson
Park

**HUDSON
SQUARE**

Charles St

Christopher St

Grove
Court

Carlton St

4th St

West 11th St

Bleecker St

St Luke's in
the Fields

Greenwich St

Washington St

Bank St

Hudson St

W Houston St

Greenwich St

West 10th St

Barrow St

Morton St

West St

Clarkson St

West 12th St

Washington St

**WEST
VILLAGE**

Bethune St

Jane St

Joe Dimaggio Highway

West St

0   150m   N

L

The Village Vanguard (178 Seventh Avenue South at Perry Street, www.villagevanguard.com), one of the world's most famous jazz clubs, open for more than 70 years and run today by founder Max Gordon's widow, Lorraine Gordon.

While The Knicks are not always fun to watch, the street ballers at West 4 Street Courts at Sixth Avenue never disappoint.

If you're in the mood to have a stronger drink than a coffee, pay tribute to Dylan Thomas' demise at the White Horse Tavern (567 Hudson Street at 11th Street, 212 243 9260), slip through the back door at one-time speakeasy Chumley's (86 Bedford Street at Barrow Street, 212 675 4449), hunker down like an old sailor at one of the oldest bars in the city, The Ear Inn (326 Spring Street at Greenwich Avenue, 212 226 9060), or throw some darts with NYU co-eds at Kettle of Fish (59 Christopher Street at Seventh Avenue, 212 414 2278).

There are endless dining options in the West Village. Grab a quick bite at hole-in-the-wall Mamoun's Falafel (119 MacDougal Street at West 3rd Street), where the pita sandwiches really are not half bad – and very, very cheap. 'Gastropub' Spotted Pig (314 West 11th Street at Greenwich

Village Shopping

Shopping opportunities abound, with chain stores and boutiques alike. Broadway Panhandler (65 East 8th Street at Broadway) sells everything a home chef needs. Flight 001 (96 Greenwich Avenue at Jane Street) has the goods for a stylish traveller, and neighbouring Mxyplyzyk (125 Greenwich Avenue at 13th Street) has jewellery, housewares, and gifts that make up for the tongue-twister name.

Avenue, 212 620 0393) is overrun with customers on the weekends, hungry for the Michelin-starred British and Italian fare. Blue Hill (75 Washington Place at MacDougal Street, 212 539 1776), Five Points (31 Great Jones Street at Lafayette Street, 212 253 5700), and Home (20 Cornelia Street at West 4th Street, 212 243 9579) all serve stellar seasonal menus while Blue Ribbon Bakery (33 Downing Street at Bedford Street, 212 337 0404) is great for groups. There is often a line out the door at Tomoe Sushi (172 Thompson Street at Houston Street, 212 777 9346) and burger joint Corner Bistro on West 4th at Horatio Street (p.247) so time your visit wisely. Tea & Sympathy (Greenwich Avenue at 13th Street) has mastered cosy English comfort food and Pearl Oyster Bar (18 Cornelia Street at West 4th Street, 212 691 8211) is the best place to get a New England lobster roll outside of Boston.

Washington Square Park
West 4th St & University Pl   www.washingtonsquarepark.org
Once a potter's field (a graveyard for the poor) and a military parade ground, today Washington Square is the centre of New York University's campus and a prime place to people-watch. Its longstanding tradition of non-conformity fits in perfectly with the neighbourhood's bohemian do-as-you-please feel and the fountain is a major attraction for visitors big and small during the sticky summer months. The arch was erected first out of plaster and wood in 1888 to celebrate the centennial of George Washington's inauguration as the first president of the United States. The arch was then rebuilt in 1892 out of marble, and stands a grand 77 feet (23 metres) high. The park is currently under hot debate regarding its reconstruction. Map L **1**

If you only do one thing in...
West Village

Queue up at Magnolia Bakery (401 Bleecker St) for one of their coveted cupcakes. It's well worth the wait.

Best for...

Eating: Copy the *Sex and the City* girls and dine at Sushi Samba 7 (p.248) – they serve an intriguing combination of Latin and Japanese cuisine.

Drinking: Mingle with the beautiful people over a superbly mixed cocktail at Employees Only (p.250).

Sightseeing: Put away your map and wander randomly – with tree-lined streets, attractive brownstones and an eclectic mix of shops, this is a great area to get lost in.

Shopping: Explore your secret fetish with a visit to the cheeky store Leather Man (111 Christopher Street, 212 243 5339).

Outdoor: Hang out with some NYU students in Washington Square.

Other Areas

Manhattan provides an almost endless list of things to see and do. Beyond its boundaries, however, is a collection of attractions as diverse as they are interesting.

The Bronx Zoo
2300 Southern Blvd, The Bronx

718 367 1010
www.bronxzoo.com

This world-famous zoo first opened its gates in 1899. A pioneer in the use of natural habitats in the 1940s, today it houses more than 4,000 animals from around the world in specially designed exhibitions. Highlights include interacting with friendly primates in the 6.5 acre Congo Gorilla Forest, watching the Siberian cats on Tiger Mountain, seeing the small primates swing through the vines of Jungle World's recreation of an Asian rainforest, and finding the snow leopards and red pandas hiding in the Himalayan Highlands. Admission is $14 for adults, $12 for seniors, $10 for children 2-12, free for children under 2, and free for all on Wednesdays. There is an additional fee for the carousel and Congo Gorilla Forest. Open daily year round. Parking is available.

Brooklyn Botanic Garden
900 Washington Avenue, Brooklyn

718 623 7200
www.bbg.org

This garden in Prospect Park is a worthy alternative to the New York Botanic Garden, with a stunning Japanese hill and pond, charming Children's Garden, and unique Fragrance Garden among many excellent plant collections. Visitors come from all over the city for the annual Sakura Matsuri (Cherry Blossom Festival) each spring, when artists and performers from Japan entertain and educate alongside more than 200 cherry trees in glorious bloom. It is open throughout the year, except for Mondays. Admission is free on Tuesdays, Saturdays before noon, and daily mid-November through February. All other times admission is $5 for adults, $3 for student and seniors and free for children under 12.

Brooklyn Bridge

A National Historic Landmark, the Brooklyn Bridge is one of the city's most recognisable structures. It was the longest suspension bridge in the world when it began carrying traffic between Manhattan and Brooklyn in 1883. Don't leave New York without admiring this engineering marvel up close with a sunset stroll over the pedestrian walkway. History buffs will love the series of plaques that tell the remarkable story of its construction, and everyone will love the sweeping skyline view.

Brooklyn Museum of Art   718 638 5000
200 Eastern Pkwy, Brooklyn   www.brooklynmuseum.org

One of the oldest and largest museums in America, the BMA has a vast permanent collection including art and design that spans the ancient and modern history of the Americas, Europe, Asia, Africa, and the Middle East. The temporary exhibitions are world class, competing with likes of the Met and MoMA for art lovers' attention. It would take several hours to see everything, but the highlights can be condensed into two well-planned hours. Tours are regularly available and audio tours are offered at all times. Admission is $8 for adults, $4 for seniors and students, and free for children under 12.

Coney Island & Brighton Beach

718 946 1350

West 37th St to Corbin Pl   www.coneyislandusa.com

Coney Island is New York's most famous . No visit is complete without a stop at Nathan's Famous Hot Dogs, host of the nationally-televised July 4th Hot Dog Eating Contest, and a ride on the landmark wooden rollercoaster, The Cyclone. Visitors of all ages will enjoy the displays at the New York State Aquarium. For a more relaxing day by the sea, stroll down to Brighton Beach. The neighbourhood's large Russian population has earned it the nickname 'Little Odessa,' so expect sunbathers to include svelte ice blonds and babushka-wearing grannies alike. Boardwalk restaurants serve traditional Russian meals, complete with vodka by the bottle. Facilities at the beaches include food concessions, amusements, bathrooms, showers, and changing areas.

El Museo del Barrio

212 831 7272

1230 Fifth Ave, Spanish Harlem   www.elmuseo.org

This museum in Spanish Harlem, also known as El Barrio, displays both permanent and temporary exhibitions devoted to the cultures of Spanish-speaking immigrants from Puerto Rico, the Caribbean, and the Americas. The permanent collection includes artefacts from pre-Columbian indigenous cultures and an array of traditional arts and crafts, as well as painting, drawing, sculpture, photography, and film by Latino artists. Many educational programmes and special events celebrating Latino culture occur throughout the year, the most popular being the Three Kings Day Parade in early January. Admission is $4 for adults, seniors and students, and free for children under 12.

Ellis Island National Monument
212 269 5755
Ellis Island
www.nps.gov/elis
From 1892 to 1954, more than 12 million people passed through the Ellis Island Immigration Center on their way to new lives as Americans. According to the National Park Service, which operates the American Family Immigration History Center on the site today, more than 40% of Americans have an ancestor recorded here.

Fisher Landau Center
718 937 0727
38-27 30th St, Queens
www.flcart.org
This small museum has an impressive collection of contemporary art from 1960 to the present, including work by Frank Gehry, Jenny Holzer, Robert Rauschenberg, Kiki Smith, Cy Twombly, and Andy Warhol. An hour is enough to see everything, including temporary exhibits. It is open

every day from midday until 17:00, except on Tuesdays and Wednesdays when it is closed. Admission is free.

Historic Richmondtown

718 351 1611

441 Clark Ave   www.historicrichmondtown.org

This is a living history museum where costumed guides inhabit a complex of 15 buildings, depicting life in New York from the colonial era to the present. A mix of demonstrations and hands-on activities is designed to appeal to visitors of all ages. There are tours daily, and guides are stationed inside most of the buildings. Admission is $5 for adults, $4 for seniors, $3.50 for students, and free for children under 5.

Manhattan Beach

718 946 1373

Oriental Blvd from Ocean Ave to Mackenzie St

This small beach isn't far from the action at Coney Island, but it feels a world away. It has a large picnic area shaded by trees, making it a popular spot for families with young children looking to celebrate special occasions by the sea. Facilities include basketball and tennis courts, barbecue grills, bathrooms, showers and changing areas.

Museum of the Moving Image

718 784 4520

36-01 35th Ave, Queens   www.movingimage.us

This museum is dedicated to films, videos, digital media, and the technology behind making them, with hands-on displays showing how moving images are made. Kids will love the exhibit that allows visitors to create their own flipbook, made available for purchase in the gift shop. Screenings of classic films are held several times a week, as are top-notch festivals dedicated to the work of individual directors, actors, and writers. Previews and premieres of new films, and talks by the people who make them, are a regular treat. Admission is $10 for adults, $7.50 for seniors and students, $5 for children under 18, free for children under 5.

The New York Aquarium   718 265 3474
Surf Ave & West 8th St, Brooklyn   www.nyaquarium.com
The city's only aquarium displays 350 different species housed in a variety of indoor and outdoor displays. Look inside for colourful Caribbean fish, eerily beautiful jellyfish and menacing sharks, then head outside to watch the playful antics of the walrus, otters, sea lions, and penguins. There is an indoor cafe and several food carts should you get the munchies. The aquarium is open daily all year round. Admission is $12 for adults, $8 for seniors, $8 for children 2-12, and free for children under 2.

New York Botanic Garden   718 817 8700
Bronx River Pkwy, The Bronx   www.nybg.org
The city's premier botanical garden has been growing since 1891. Its 250 acres are a National Historic Landmark housing 50 garden and plant collections, America's largest Victorian glass

house, and several historic buildings. Popular annual events at the garden include the world class Orchid Show in early spring, and the Holiday Train Show in December, when city streetscapes are reproduced in foliage. It is open throughout the year, every day except Mondays. Admission prices vary.

New York Hall of Science

718 699 0005

47-01 111th St, Queens

www.nyscience.org

With hands-on exhibits designed to teach kids about everything from microbes to rocket science, this museum is a must for primary school-age children. Audio tours are available at all times, and specialised tours and workshops are regularly scheduled. Admission is $11 for adults, $8 for students and seniors, and free for children under 2.

New York Transit Museum

718 694 1600

Boerum Pl, Brooklyn

www.mta.info/mta/museum

The Metropolitan Transportation Authority's museum is dedicated to the city's transportation networks, with exhibits of artefacts, photographs, posters, and art designed to appeal to both kids and adults. The whole thing can be seen in about an hour and a half. The gift shop has tonnes of fun New York souvenirs, with a branch on site here and another conveniently located inside Grand Central Terminal. Admission to the museum is $5 for adults, $3 for students and seniors, and free for children under 3.

The Noguchi Museum

718 204 7088
9-01 33rd Rd, Queens
www.noguchi.org

This museum is dedicated to the work of Japanese-American artist Isamu Noguchi, housing a permanent collection of his sculptures and home designs in a beautifully restored factory site. The whole museum can be seen in about an hour, but visitors often linger in the serene courtyard. Tours are given daily, and a number of educational programmes are held on a regular basis. Admission is $10 for adults, $5 for seniors and students, and free for children under 12.

Orchard Beach

718 885 2275
On the Long Island Sound in Pelham Bay Park

Built in the 1930s, 'The Bronx Riviera' has always been popular with local residents. Weekend crowds can be large, but weekdays are usually quiet. Facilities include a central pavilion with shops and food concessions, bathrooms, showers and changing areas, playgrounds, basketball, volleyball and handball courts, picnic areas, and parking. They also run free events for kids, such as owl watching, searching for songbirds and watching for waterfowl.

P.S. 1

718 784 2084
22-25 Jackson Ave, Long Island City
www.ps1.org

Think of P.S.1 as MoMA's younger, hipper sister. While its famous sibling shows the work of the 20th century's greatest artists, P.S.1 shows new art that has not made it onto a postcard yet. All exhibitions are temporary and they change frequently, so check with the museum to see what is on view. It can take several hours to visit every room in P.S.1 and the sprawling floor plan demands the use of a map. Admission is $5 for adults, $2 for seniors and students, and free for children under 12 or with a MoMA ticket dated in the past 30 days. During summer, P.S.1 hosts Warm Up every Saturday: a series of parties that attract world-famous DJs and huge crowds to the museum's courtyard.

Prospect Park

718 965 8951
Parkside Ave, Brooklyn   www.prospectpark.org

This is Brooklyn's answer to Central Park, quite literally, since the 585 acre space was created by the same duo that designed and made Central Park. Built in 1867 the park has since grown to encompass plenty of meadows, forests, and trails, plus a lake, a skating rink, a zoo, and a large farmers' market on the weekends. The park has always been considered a work of art, from its very inception and revolutionary style to the colourful creatures that wander the small plot of wilderness, slap bang in the heart of Brooklyn.

Prospect Park Zoo

718 399 7339
450 Flatbush Ave   www.nyzoosandaquarium.com

Brooklyn's small zoo has three exhibition areas specially designed for kids, where young visitors can pet farm animals, get up close with some wild species, and learn about zoology and wildlife conservation. The zoo is open daily all year round. Admission is $6 for adults, $2.25 for seniors, $2 for children up to 3-12, and free for children under 3.

Queens Botanical Garden   718 886 3800
43-50 Main St, Queens   www.queensbotanical.org

This garden began as a display for the 1939 World's Fair, and today its focus is on connecting horticulture with the diverse ethnic cultures of Queens. Major renovations were completed in spring 2007, yielding a number of innovative landscapes and buildings designed with environmental preservation in mind. Open year round, the garden is closed Mondays. Parking is available and admission is free.

Queens Museum of Art   718 592 9700
Flushing Meadows-Corona Park   www.queensmuseum.org

The QMA's quirky permanent collection includes materials from the two World's Fairs held on its site, crime scene photographs from the New York Daily News archives, and artist William Sharps' drawings of New York streetscapes. Temporary exhibitions of contemporary art are held throughout the year. Everything can be seen in about an hour and a half. The museum's most famous attraction is the Panorama of the City of New York, a scale model of the entire city with 895,000 distinct structures. Admission is $5 for adults, $2.50 for seniors and students, and free for children under 5.

Queens Zoo

53-51 111th St

718 271 1500
www.nyzoosandaquarium.com

This zoo has a unique collection consisting only of animals native to north and south America. This is the place to come if you want to catch up with the animals that feature in American heritage. While the animals inhabit natural landscapes, the birds are housed in a geodesic dome designed by Buckminster Fuller for the 1964 World's Fair. Queens Zoo is open daily all year round. Admission is $6 for adults, $2.25 for seniors, $2 for children 3-12 and free for children under 3.

Rockaway Beach

From Beach 1st St to Beach 149th St

718 318 4000

Rockaway is the city's largest beach at about seven miles long, and on its east side neighbours a National Park Service beach at Jacob Riis Park. Immortalised in The Ramones' hit song Rockaway Beach, it is best known for having the only designated surfing area in New York. The sand gets crowded near subway stops, but remains fairly quiet elsewhere, even on the weekends. Facilities include a small boardwalk with shops and food concessions, playgrounds, basketball and handball courts, bathrooms and changing areas. Birdwatchers won't want to miss the chance to visit nearby Rockaway Arverne Shorebird Preserve and the Rockaway Beach Endangered Species Nesting Area.

Schomburg Center for Research in Black Culture
212 491 2200

515 Lenox Ave, Harlem   www.nypl.org/research/sc

This branch of the New York Public Library is a cultural centre built around an archive of 10 million items relating to the history and culture of the worldwide African diaspora. The collection includes books, manuscripts, art, artefacts, films, audio recordings, photographs, and prints, displayed in special exhibitions curated by the library. Admission is free.

South & Midland Beaches
718 816 6804

Lower New York Bay from Fort Wadsworth to Miller Field, Staten Island

This clean and well-maintained beach is far less crowded than others around town, with calm waters ideal for young swimmers. Facilities in the recently renovated park include a small boardwalk/promenade, playgrounds, baseball fields, handball, shuffleboard, bocce, basketball courts, a skateboard park, a roller hockey rink, a fishing pier, food concessions, bathrooms, a ramp for wheelchair access and parking.

The Staten Island Botanical Garden
718 273 8200

1000 Richmond Terrace   www.sibg.org

This garden boasts several unique attractions, including the Sensory Garden designed for the physically challenged, the Tuscan Garden modelled on traditional Italian landscaping, and the Connie Gretz Secret Garden – a reproduction of an

18th century European garden maze. The highlight is the New York Chinese Scholar's Garden; a classical painting brought to life in a series of landscaped walkways and pavilions encircling a pond. The garden is open year round. Admission is free for the Botanical Garden, $5 for the Chinese Scholar's Garden and Secret Garden ($4 for children, students, and seniors), and $2 for the Secret Garden alone, but children and adults accompanying children are free.

Staten Island Zoo

614 Broadway, Staten Island

718 442 3100
www.statenislandzoo.org

This small zoo won't impress adults, but it has lots of activities for families. There is a great variety of fish, amphibians and reptiles on display, and a limited collection of birds and mammals, such as meerkats, leopards, red pandas, bushbabies and groundhogs. It is open daily throughout the year. Admission is $7 for adults, $5 for seniors, $4 for children 3-14, and free for children under 3.

Statue of Liberty National Monument

Liberty Island

212 363 3200
www.nps.gov/stli

The Statue of Liberty, originally called 'Liberty Enlightening the World', was a gift from the French to mark the 100 year anniversary of America's independence from the British. This New York icon has stood watch over the harbour since 1886; a symbol of freedom for the millions of immigrants arriving at nearby Ellis Island. The statue stands at 305 feet high (from the ground to the tip of the torch) on a pedestal in the shape of an 11 pointed star. Take a ferry from Battery Park to visit Lady Liberty, or join the crowd getting a good look from afar by taking the Staten Island Ferry (free of charge) and bagging a seat on the west-facing deck.

Wave Hill

West 249th St & Independence Ave

718 549 3200
www.wavehill.org

Built as a private estate in 1843, Wave Hill is set in one of the city's most beautiful landscapes. Famous former residents include President Theodore Roosevelt and novelist Mark Twain. The gardens and cultural centre are open year round, but closed on Mondays. Admission is free on Tuesdays, Saturdays before noon, and daily December through February. All other times admission is $4 for adults, $2 for student and seniors, free for children under 6.

Wolfe's Pond Beach

Raritan Bay

718 984 8266

This beach is almost always calm and quiet, surrounded by a Forever Wild Nature Preserve. A perfect place to hike and swim in a single afternoon, with plenty of wildlife, such as hermit and blue crabs and blue mussels. Facilities include playgrounds, picnic areas, bathrooms, ramps for wheelchair accessibility, and parking.

Tours

There are thousands of things to see in New York, and various ways to see them. A guided tour can highlight the essential attractions and provide a unique perspective.

There are sightseeing tours to suit every need: short-term visitors can do tours that hit many popular sights in one day, while those with more time may prefer to focus in on particular neighbourhoods or attractions. Further information on local tours can be found on www.nycvisit.com.

Bicycle Tours

Bike The Big Apple
201 837 1133
1306 Second Ave   www.bikethebigapple.com
These bike tours entail about four to five hours of riding on routes in Manhattan, Brooklyn, Queens, and the Bronx. Both bikes and helmets are provided.

Central Park Bicycle Tours/Rentals
212 541 8759
2 Columbus Circle   www.centralparkbiketour.com
This company offers a two hour bike tour of Central Park. Bikes are provided, and bike rentals for personal use are available as well.

Boat Tours

Circle Line
212 269 5755
17 Battery Pl, Suite 715 www.circlelinedowntown.com

Downtown harbour routes leave from the South Street Seaport (see www.circlelinedowntown.com), while ferries headed for Liberty and Ellis Islands depart from Battery Park. From the West Side, tour options include a three-hour circumnavigation of Manhattan and a two-hour semi-circle around lower Manhattan.

New York Water Taxi
212 742 1969
499 Van Brunt St, Section 8B www.nywatertaxi.com

This company's yellow-chequered boats zip through the harbour, ferrying both commuters and sightseers alike. In addition to guided tours, passengers can purchase two-day passes that allow them to hop on and hop off at terminals in Midtown and the Financial District, Williamsburg and Red Hook in Brooklyn, and Long Island City in Queens.

NY Waterway
201 902 8700
350 Fifth Ave, Suite 610 www.nywaterway.com

This company caters to both residents and tourists, with routes between Manhattan and New Jersey and a number of tour options. It is best known for its 90 minute Happy Hour cruises and two hour Party Tours, where the skyline becomes a backdrop for drinks and dancing.

Bus Tours

Gray Line New York
212 445 0848

Various hop-on locations www.newyorksightseeing.com

There's not much you won't see on this tour. You can take the Downtown loop, which will take you past the Empire State Building, the Flatiron Building, Greenwich Village, Soho, Washington Square Park, through Little Italy and Chinatown, past City Hall, down Wall Street, up through the East Village, past the UN Headquarters and the Rockefeller Center, around Madison Square Garden and into Times Square. Alternatively, take the Uptown loop and head for the Lincoln Center, Central Park, the posh Upper West Side, Harlem Market, the Guggenheim, the Met and the Apollo Theater. Pay a special price and you can ride both loops for up to three days, hopping on and off at will. There's also a Brooklyn loop, leaving every 30 minutes from the South Street Seaport.

Culinary Tours

Foods of New York Tours
212 209 3370

Various locations www.foodsofny.com

Eating and walking, walking and eating – these tours take you on a stroll through some of the city's most characteristic neighbourhoods – find all the best eateries in Greenwich Village, the Chelsea Market and the MeatPacking District, and Soho, with plenty of tasting along the way.

New York Chocolate Tours

917 292 0680
www.sweetwalks.com

Various locations

Candy lovers can choose from one of two routes: one exploring a few upscale chocolate shops and another that stops in the newest local boutiques. Fortunately, all the walking burns off at least a few of the calories.

Savory Sojourns

212 691 7314
www.savorysojourns.com

155 West 13th St

This company has 20 tour itineraries, covering more than a dozen neighbourhoods in Manhattan plus Atlantic Avenue and DUMBO in Brooklyn and Arthur Avenue in the Bronx.

Helicopter & Plane Tours

Helicopter Flight Services Inc

212 355 0801
www.heliny.com

Pier 6 and the East River

Fly over Manhattan and the harbour for 15 to 30 minutes, or take a 30 minute private charter starting at $1,350 for up to six passengers. They also offer additional services, such as airport transfers, flight training and aerial photography.

Liberty Helicopters Inc.

212 967 2099
libertyhelicopters.com

424 West 33rd St, Suite 510

These helicopter tours over Manhattan and the harbour run up to 17 minutes long. Tours cost as little as $30 for the shortest tour, which lasts just two minutes – it simply goes up and comes down again. Additional tours depart from Paulus Hook Pier on the waterfront in Jersey City, New Jersey.

Heritage Tours

Harlem Spirituals/New York Visions
690 Eighth Ave , 2nd floor

212 391 0900
www.harlemspirituals.com

This company specialises in heritage bus tours of African-American communities in Harlem, Brooklyn, and the Bronx. Some itineraries offer a special focus on jazz and gospel music, soul food restaurants, or historic landmarks.

Joyce Gold History Tours of NY
141 West 17th St

212 242 5762
www.nyctours.com

An author and professor at New York University and the New School gives walking tours focusing on the history of various Manhattan neighbourhoods. Tours last around two and a half hours, and cost around $15, depending on the tour.

Timeline Touring
2015 Kings Highway

718 339 2302
www.timelinetouring.com

This company offers public and private walking tours that focus exclusively on the Jewish history of the Lower East Side. Visit kosher delis, a historic tenement, and a landmark synagogue.

Sightseeing & Shopping Tours

Bridge and Tunnel Club Tours
347 323 4321
Various Locations   info@bridgeandtunnelclub.com

A historian and a travel writer share their passion for exploring their city on tours to locations in all five boroughs. All itineraries are customised and can include stops for sightseeing, shopping, athletics, and dining.

Elegant Tightwad Shopping Excursions
516 735 2085
Various Locations   www.theeleganttightwad.com

Take a tour of designer showrooms and sample sales in the Garment District, the Upper East Side, and downtown. Tours cost between $45 and $145 per person, depending on the size of your group and the itinerary. It includes about four hours of shopping, a book full of shopping tips, and a list of other shops and sales to discover once the tour is over.

Shop Gotham
866 795 4200
Various Locations   www.shopgotham.com

This highly recommended company covers Nolita, Soho, the Garment District, and Fifth Avenue. Prices differ according to area, but most tours will take you into wholesale showrooms that are open exclusively to tour members, as well as some of those famous (yet hard to find) sample sales.

Sports & Spas

Sports and Activities

New York may work hard, but it plays hard too – from cycling and golf to dancing and sailing, there's plenty of action to be had.

When you get bored with the museums, and your cards are maxed out from all the shopping, New York still has lots to offer. Its wide expanses of greenery attract runners, walkers, rollerbladers and cyclists throughout the year, as well as many other sports fans. And in a city of eight million people, it's pretty easy to get a group together for the team sport of your choice – you don't even have to know your team mates: spend a sunny afternoon in the park and you'll probably get countless invites to join in on a game of volleyball, soccer, or frisbee.

New York is a city with definite weather changes from season to season, offering sweltering sunshine in summer and icy cold blizzards in winter. As the seasons change, so does the emphasis on particular sports. So in summer you can expect bicycle races and watersports, and during winter you can ice skate in the Rockefeller Center or Bryant Park (see p.87 for more information on ice skating). Spring is great for sailing along the Long Island Sound, while summertime brings bicycle races and marathons. In spring you can enjoy boating trips along the Long Island Sound, and fall marks the beginning of baseball season.

Central Park Activities

Of course New York wouldn't be the city it is if you couldn't do something a bit off-the-wall. For an adrenaline-rushed view of the city from above, the licensed instructors at Skydive The Ranch (845 255 4033, www.skydivetheranch.com) can arrange for you to do a tandem skydive. For an added fee you can have your jump recorded and then transferred to either VHS or DVD so that you can watch your descent over and over again – now that's a great holiday memory! There's also paintball, where you can shoot your friends or family with little plastic bombs filled with paint (and, of course, they can shoot you right back). Cousins Paintball (800 352 4007, www.cousinspaintball.com) has three locations in New York.

If your idea of a good sport is a little less exhilarating, and you have time in your schedule, you can take part in some of America's most famous sports. If you fancy shooting some hoops, just head down to the courts on West 3rd Street (on the corner of Sixth Avenue). You'll usually find casual games in progress and you could be that extra

Watersports

New York is famous for its traffic jams, but its waterways can get pretty clogged up too. Most watersports require lots of open space and as little marine traffic as possible, so it's better to head over to the Long Island Sound – at least there you'll get your adrenaline rush from performing some gravity-defying tricks, and not from playing chicken with a commercial freighter. You'll find plenty of places along the Sound where you can hire a boat.

player they needed. These courts are also used for the growing sport of American handball.

At Chelsea Piers (16th to 23rd Street, Chelsea, 212 336 6666) you can partake in numerous sports, including bowling, air hockey, mini basketball, golf, rock climbing, volleyball and ice hockey.

For some serene greenery, take a trip to Central Park. You can arrange for a horse-drawn carriage to take you round, walk along shaded paths, go for a jog, rollerblade, or come the season, don your skates and hit the ice. The Wollman Rink (212 439 6900, www.wollmanskatingrink.com) hires out skates for $5 on payment of an admission fee. Other outdoor skating rinks (they usually open around the end of October) include the Rink at Rockefeller Plaza (www.therinkatrockcenter.com) and the Pond at Bryant Park (www.bryantpark.org). You can also skate throughout the year at the Chelsea Piers Sky Rink (212 336 6100).

Horse-drawn carriage in Central Park

Golf

People travel the world to play golf, and despite being a heaving metropolis of busy streets and giant skyscrapers, New York has its fair share of greens.

If you're interested in playing on the same course as some of the world's top professionals, then you're in luck. Or if you just happen to be looking for the largest public golf facility in the world, then you're in luck too! New York's golf courses offer a little bit of everything – from tricky terrain to long, flat greens .

The Oak Hill Country Club (www.oakhillcc.com) in Rochester has a long history of hosting major championships, including the US open in 1989, the Ryder Cup in 1995, and the PGA Championship in 2003. Ben Hogan was one of the first big names to play there, and in 1942 he shot a round of 64, which remains the course record to this day. History was made in 2002 when the famous Black Course at Long Island's Bethpage State Park (www.bethpagecommunity.com) became the first ever public course to host the US Open. Tiger Woods took the trophy that day; Bethpage will host the Open once again in 2009.

If you're in town and fancy a round, The Golf Academy at Chelsea Piers (212 336 6444, www.chelseapiers.com) is easily accessible or try Kissena Golf Course in Queens (718 939 4594, http://kissena.e-golf.net) for some challenging shots and breathtaking views of Manhattan.

Chelsea Piers

Spectator Sports

Tap into the passion of New Yorkers at an action-packed match or game, where celebrities and fans mingle courtside to cheer on their teams.

Major sports like baseball, American football, basketball and hockey provide year-round excitement. Tickets for sporting events can usually be purchased at stadiums, team websites, or through TicketMaster (www.ticketmaster.com), unless it's a major event that sells out quickly. Since New York is teeming with sports fans, you will find that this happens pretty often, so it's best to plan ahead, and to purchase tickets as early as possible. Don't buy tickets from scalpers on the street, no matter how tempting. It's illegal, the prices are inflated, and the chances of buying a fake ticket and being denied entry at the gate are high.

American Football

Fast-moving, action-packed with plenty of bone-crunching pile-ups – American Football is not for the faint hearted. It's a thrilling sport and if you're in town at Thanksgiving you'll catch the excitment of the biggest game on the calendar: the Super Bowl. Both the Giants (www.giants.com) and the Jets (www.newyorkjets.com) play home games in the Meadowlands Sports Complex in New Jersey.

Baseball

Baseball is big business in the Big Apple. It is home to the mighty Mets (http://newyork.mets.mlb.com) and the Yankees (http://newyork.yankees.mlb.com) – two teams with intense rivalry between them, and one of the ultimate legends of the game – the late, great Babe Ruth.

Basketball

As soon as you set foot in New York you're bound to hear someone mention the Knicks – New York's favourite basketball team play their home games in Madison Square Garden. For more information see www.nba.com/knicks.

Ice Hockey

Catch the thrills of a game of either New York's home teams, the New York Islanders (516 501 6700, www.newyorkislanders.com) and the New York Rangers (212 465 6000, www.newyorkrangers.com).

Spas & Nail Bars

There's nothing like a soothing spa treatment after a day of hard shopping in New York. Treat yourself – you know you deserve it...

At the end of a hustly-bustly New York day, it's finally time for some TLC. Forget the bright city lights and the super-busy streets, and relax for a few blissful hours. New York does luxury well and is full of luxurious spas to suit every taste and budget. Disappear into the soothing sanctum of one of them, and you'll emerge revitalised and ready to take on the city with renewed vigour. Day spas are particularly popular, and the newest trend is the 'medispa', where clinical treatments such as laser lifts, collagen and botox are offered alongside the more pleasurable wraps and facials. Most spas offer packages where you can enjoy several treatments at a lower price. And if you'd like to share the experience with your honey, bond over a couples' massage, available at many outlets.

Acqua Beauty Bar

212 620 4329

7 East 14th St, Union Square   www.acquabeautybar.com

For a taste of paradise, Asian style, head to the peaceful Acqua Beauty Bar and treat your face to a botanical purifying facial. Or try the 'Garden of Eastern Delights', which includes a shiatsu massage and a mist facial. Top it off with an Indonesian 'ritual of beauty' where your skin is scrubbed with ground rice and kneaded with fragrant oils.

Affinia Wellness Spa
The Benjamin Hotel, Midtown

212 715 2517
www.thebenjamin.com

Affinia is all about relaxation and harmony, and the treatments are tailored to the New York demographic – pressed-for-time professionals – with such treatments as the 'shopper's relief' for weary feet and calves. The massages are so dreamy that you may find it hard to stop at just one. The East meets West massage combines Shiatsu and acupressure, while the deep Swedish massage will leave your body tingling from your scalp to your toes.

Bliss
568 Broadway, Soho

212 219 8970
www.blissworld.com

Saunter through the spa and pick your pampering, like a carrot and sesame body buff, a hot salt scrub or a super

blissage, a full-body massage like no other. Bliss also offers 'groom service' for the guys, including the cheekily named 'homme improvement', an energising facial, including blackhead eliminations. Their manis and pedis are pure decadence: go for the hot milk and almond or double chocolate pedicure. You'll also find Bliss on 57th Street and on Lexington Avenue.

Cornelia Day Resort
663 Fifth Ave, Midtown

212 871 3050
www.cornelia.com

The reigning queen of New York's day spas has set the bar – and high – for her competitors. Rising over Fifth Avenue, the swank resort boasts a relaxation 'library' with soft leather couches, champagne and nibbles like grapes on toothpicks, and a sun-kissed roof garden with soaking baths. Deep-cleansing facials – with exfoliation and extractions – are customised to suit your skin, and incorporate vitamins, plant proteins and antioxidants.

Four Seasons Hotel Spa
57 East 57th St, Midtown

212 758 5711
www.fourseasons.com

This spa is pure luxury. The massage menu, for starters, leaves you spoiled for choice, including the signature therapeutic massage – shiatsu, aromatherapy, Thai and reflexology. Try the 'Four Seasons in One' treatment, with four pamper cycles, each related to a season of the year. Suffering from jet lag? Revive yourself with their jet lag special, with hydrating gels and an ayurvedic scalp massage.

Great Jones Spa

212 505 3185

29 Great Jones St, Nolita   www.greatjonesspa.com

Who says the granola crowd doesn't need pampering? The haute-hippie Great Jones Spa, with its organic purifications, chakra-light steam room and raw-food cafe, appeals to the bohemian-chic brigade who may shudder at the thought of processed anything, but aren't opposed to a lavender footbath and pedicure.

Haven Spa

212 343 3515

150 Mercer St, Soho

Haven's creative spa menu includes the Body & Sol (exfoliation and sunless tanning), the Forbidden Fruit (a lemon scrub followed by a lather in fruity emollient cream) and the perennially popular Hot Chocolate (with a warm milk mask and a gentle application of chocolate hydrating cream). Indulge in the Haven Foot Renaissance, a foot facial extraordinaire with a luxurious hydrating wrap and a moisturising massage.

The J Sisters

212 750 2485

35 West 57th St, Midtown   www.jsisters.com

This is the brainchild of seven Brazilian-born sisters who made their name with their excellent waxings, which are relatively pain free and long lasting. The full-leg wax brings new meaning to smooth and the popular Brazilian wax is perfect for your itty-bitty bikini. Threading, a fast, effective method of hair removal, is also available. The J Sisters also offer superb facials, manicures and pedicures.

Juva MediSpa
60 East 56th St, Midtown

212 688 5882
www.juvaskin.com

Juva offers a full range of physician-formulated treatments, including chemical peels, eyelifts and laser procedures. A facial here is a two-hour-plus ritual that includes careful extractions, a hydrating mask and a sonic brush scrub. Curious about Botox? This pioneering spot is the place to do it. An extensive consultation is the first step, and the injections are adjusted to fit the needs of the patient, so there's no danger of the 'frozen look.'

Mario Badescu
320 East 52nd St, Midtown

212 758 1065
www.mariobadescu.com

Celebrities adore super-stylist Mario Badescu, whose facials and body scrubs, made with fresh fruits, are as popular as his products. Badescu's potions blend medical properties with lavish lotions, like a creamy collagen cream or a hydro-moisturiser infused with Vitamin C. Before walking out with your beauty bounty, head into the relaxing salon and indulge in a reflexology massage. Steady pressure is applied to points in the feet that correspond to different body parts and organs, which facilitates the flow of energy and eases tension.

Essential Therapy
122 East 25th St, Gramercy

212 777 2325
www.essentialtherapyny.com

Frequented by the celeb set, Essential Therapy boasts the finest massages in the city, designed to provide long-lasting therapeutic results. Alleviate chronic tension with the deep-tissue massage; feel the warmth from hot stones penetrate the entire curvature of your back; relieve your weary neck and back with a craniosacral therapy session; and increase flexibility and reduce pressure on joints with stretching sessions.

Graceful Services
1097 Second Ave, Midtown

212 593 9904
www.gracefulservices.com

This place focuses on the art of massage, pure and simple. Give in to a 'four hands' session, when two deft therapists pummel your entire body into tingling submission, from your scalp to the balls of your feet; indulge in a deep-tissue massage – Chinese, Swedish or Shiatsu; or try the invigorating Guasha, where a piece of bull's horn is scraped along the spine to release tension. Prices start at $50 for a 45 minute massage.

Nail Bars
Having fabulous nails is practically de rigueur in New York, and with a salon or nail bar on just about every street, there's no excuse for scruffy fingers and toes. You can go high-end in opulent surroundings with beautiful interior design, or you can go for a straight-up, no-frills service in cheaper (but still good) nail bars. Artisan Spa (212 260 1338, www.artisanspa. com) in East Village and Dashing Diva (212 673 9000, www. dashingdiva.com) in the West Village are both popular spots and offer manicures from $10. Dashing Diva also offers manicures for men.

Shopping

Shopping NYC

A mind-boggling variety of quality stores, a favourable exchange rate and some serious bargains make New York City the ultimate shoppers' paradise.

Think NYC, think shopping. The city is known the world over as the place to come for serious retail-based activity. It may not be the cheapest place on earth, certainly not to live in, but the weakened dollar and the sheer range of choice means visiting shopping fans will be in consumer heaven in the Big Apple.

If it's clothes you're after, New York is well known for its love affair with fashion. New York Fashion Week (www.mbfashionweek.com/newyork) happens twice a year, and sees a flurry of famous designers gathering in Bryant Park to show off their new collections.

If you know where to look, sales and bargains can always be found. Stores such as Century 21, Filene's Basement or Loehmann's (see p.170 for more information on the city's great department stores) may require time and dedication to find the best bargains, but they make designer creations a bit more attainable. Designers' sample sales (see www.dailycandy.com and www.topbutton.com) are fantastic resources for finding luxury items at a fraction of the cost

There are bargains on everything around national holiday dates, when many stores extend their hours. On Black Friday (the day after Thanksgiving) most retailers offer big discounts to encourage early Christmas shopping, so you can anticipate both deals and crowds on this day. New York is also home to many second-hand shops (although the Manhattan ones can still be pretty pricey). Vintage clothing shops offer a range of labels in varying conditions, but they are always worth a visit – nothing can beat the feeling of finding a gorgeous vintage handbag at a bargain price.

Soho is one of the most popular areas and has a huge variety of stores – it is also jam-packed on the weekends. Nearby in Nolita, speciality boutiques and eclectic shops are gaining ground. Tribeca has a modern yet untouched feel; you might think you've strayed off course if it weren't for the excellent shopping. Along Fifth Avenue, from 50th Street and up, indulgent brands such as Louis Vuitton share street occupancy with more affordable brands like Zara and Mexx. That's the great thing about Manhattan: no matter which area you are exploring, you'll find a quirky mix of shops along the way. Sure, there are the big stores that have

Refunds & Exchanges

Store policies on refunds or exchanges can vary wildly – the best way to protect yourself is to find out what the deal is before you hand over your money. Many reputable shops will have their policy on display near the checkout counter, but if you don't see it there, be sure to ask the assistant. If the policy isn't posted in the store, then technically you are allowed to return the item within 20 days, provided it is in the original condition – so make sure you ask for a receipt.

helped make Manhattan so famous as a retail destination, but there are just as many hidden gems that seem to be a well-kept secret among stylish locals.

Further out, Woodbury Common offers exceptional outlet shopping for the diehards. Do not expect to conquer it in a day: there are more than 200 shops and returning is almost mandatory. Chanel, Gucci, Cole Haan, Tahari, Crate & Barrel, Off 5th- Saks Fifth Avenue, Fendi and Burberry are just a few of its enticing attributes. Woodbury Common is located in Central Valley, New York, and is accessible by car, bus and train. You can get a train from Penn Station, and a round-trip ticket costs less than $20. Go to www.premiumoutlets.com/woodburycommon for more details and prices.

Buying American products while you are in New York will be cheaper than in your home country – brands such as Coach, Levi's and Nike usually cost less in the US, and certain electronic items such as MP3 players, laptops and cameras are also well priced. There is no sales tax on clothing or footwear less than $110 either, with normal tax in New York City standing at 8.375%.

Shipping

The cost of shipping larger goods can sometimes exceed the cost of the item in question (especially if you bought that television for half price), but many stores can help with shipping arrangements. DHL (800 225 5345), Aramex (718 553 8740) and UPS (800 742 5877) offer international shipping. The cost of shipping any item is usually based on weight, time of arrival and destination.

Hotspots

Head downtown to Greenwich Village, Nolita, Tribeca and Noho for boutiques and indy shops, or uptown between 57th and 79th Streets for exclusive shopping and plastic-melting prices.

East Village

It has been said that much of the earthiness of New York City has departed, but the East Village is one district clinging tightly to its cool vibe. St Marks Place is home to alternative, punk and goth fashions; here you can pick up something in mesh at Trash & Vaudeville, and then dine at the quaint Café Orlin. Many fresh independent shops line 7th and 9th Streets. Women will love to stroll down 7th Street between First Avenue and Avenue A and hit Sophie Roan. On the Lower East Side the young-minded hunt for new designers in the likes of TG-170 on Ludlow, or for glam rock jewellery at Exhibitionist on Orchard Street. The Sugar Sweet Sunshine bakery nearby is great if you need to refuel.

Fifth Avenue

The Flatiron District is great for leisurely perusals, with prices that range from the moderate at trendy stores, such as Zara and Club Monaco, to the sky-high at designer label spots such as Searle and Intermix. If you've yet to be introduced to Anthropologie, it is a must for feminine clothing, accessories, and rustic homeware. Going up Fifth Avenue into Midtown

also has its advantages with high-end stores such as
Ermenegildo Zegna, Gucci and Van Cleef & Arpels servicing
bigger budgets. Sports enthusiasts looking for a customised
basketball jersey can shop at the NBA Store, while the college
set will love the beachy feel of Abercrombie & Fitch, where a
pair of men's jeans costs around $80.

The stretch of Fifth Avenue from 50th Street upwards is
a slice of retail heaven. The Apple Store (767 Fifth Avenue,
between 58th and 59th Streets, 212 336 1440) is a high-tech,
high-style shrine to Macs and iPods. It is open 24 hours, offers
free WiFi (if you're not travelling with your own laptop you
can just use any of the in-store demo models), and has great
prices on Apple products. Right next door is the ultimate
store for kids of all ages – FAO Schwarz (212 644 9400).

Meatpacking District

Stella McCartney's stellar clothing sets the tone for this
offbeat, scene-stealing area of Manhattan. Frequented
by New Yorkers and fashionistas looking for a shopping
environment not laden with tourists, the Meatpacking District
delivers a powerful one-two punch of expensive goods. Shop
in Diane von Furstenberg, Elizabeth Charles, or Jeffrey New
York, the latter of which contains selected pieces by labels
such as DSquared2 and Gucci. At Jean Shop, men, women
and kids can choose washing treatments for their one-of-
a-kind jeans cut from Japanese fabric. The disposition of
shoppers and sales associates may gravitate toward 'too cool',
so if you find yourself questioning your own adequacy, just
remember, this place is named after meat.

Soho

Soho used to be an area where street vendors sold 'hot' items with questionable origins amid artists hawking original wares on cobbled streets. But its image has changed over the years causing many shoppers to seek out its adjoining district neighbours, Nolita and Noho, where the niche shops that have been shut out of Soho have relocated. Broadway has instead become a hub for chain stores, causing some residents to long for Soho's heyday of artistic endeavours, but streets such as Wooster, Greene, Grand and West Broadway are still ripe with designer boutiques, galleries and innovative home furnishing stores. Some fantastic shops for clothing and accessories include Ted Baker, Anna Sui, and IF. Soho remains a popular shopping spot, with weekday outings offering a more pleasurable experience (you don't have to dodge the determined weekend shoppers).

Brooklyn

Brooklyn has become a beloved borough for shoppers and renters alike. Certain stores in the hipster haven of Williamsburg or in the blooming area of Park Slope have become worth the train ride out. Smith Street, running through Cobble Hill and Carroll Gardens, is one of the cooler places to shop in the city. Area Kids sells the cutest clothes for young children aged up to 8. Bird, Flirt, or Dear Fieldbinder for the ladies and Watts on Smith for the men guarantee everyone stays happy and hip. Afterward, enjoy a romantic Italian meal at Panino'teca.

Department Stores

Flagship stores such as Macy's, Bloomingdale's, Barneys, and Saks Fifth Avenue are not just places to shop – they're institutions that rival the Empire State Building and Statue of Liberty as New York's top attractions.

Perhaps because the department store phenomenon is so huge, New York has fewer malls than many other American cities. However, if the mall rat inside you needs a fix, check out the Time Warner Center (Columbus Circle, at Broadway and 59th Street, 212 823 6300).

Barneys

660 Madison Ave, Upper East Side   212 826 8900

This store is considered an underground institution and was one of Carrie Bradshaw's favourite stores in *Sex and the City*. Barneys makes you feel as if you have landed on a fabulous planet with only the finest merchandise, all a couple of hundred dollars away from being yours. Mix among label-conscious women and the occasional celebrity as they purchase beauty products from D. Sebagh, Sco, and Serge Lutens. Smelling booths are located on the lower level and feature Frederic Malle's infamous Editions de Parfums. An offshoot is Barneys Co-Op, where the flagship's seventh and eighth floors have expanded into three separate store locations in Chelsea, Soho and on the Upper West Side.

Bergdorf Goodman

754 Fifth Ave, Midtown   212 753 7300

This is haute fashion for an elite clientele. The women's store spans seven floors while the men's, across the street, sums it up in three – and both make you feel as if you have entered a private home. Labels for men include Adam Kimmel, Thom Browne, Etro, Charvet, and Alexander McQueen, while women will encounter swoon-worthy stellar clothing, decadent home goods, and $2,000 Burberry coats. You might not get immediate service from the staff at either location if you don't dress the part. And if you're trying to work out how much things cost in your local currency, don't bother – it equals a lot. Bergdorf Goodman Men is on Fifth Avenue at 58th Street.

Bloomingdale's

1000 Third Ave, Upper East Side   212 705 2000

What began as a small women's speciality shop on the Lower East Side in Manhattan is now synonymous with the city itself. 'Bloomie's' sells fine men's, women's, and children's clothing, a vast array of accessories, shoes, housewares, furniture and has a cosmetics department that prides itself on offering obscure brands. Committed and approachable salespeople abound and are eager to help even if you are working within the confines of a budget. There is an elaborate visitor centre on the first-floor balcony, complete with translators, an accommodating concierge, and a coupon with which to shop for that day.

Century 21

22 Cortland St, Financial District   212 227 9092

If you saw a Gucci skirt a while back but shuddered at the price, this shopper's goldmine offers you a second chance. Top American and European fashions can be found up to 75% off. The store is sectioned off primarily by brand, and there is little elbow room to scour the packed racks (weekdays are best, and, since it opens at 07:45, you can start early). The shoe department is hard to find, but just follow the permanent footprints on the second floor. Fitting room lines are long on weekends, but stay strong – this store is considered the ultimate in bargain shopping. There is another branch in Brooklyn (718 748 3266).

Daffy's

1311 Broadway, at 34th St, Midtown   212 736 4477

Daffy's chief location is in Herald Square, across the street from Macy's. Express elevators let you out on the seventh floor (men's wear), then descending escalators take you through an enormous amount of inexpensive (sometimes designer) clothing, shoes, lingerie, home decor accessories and incidentals. Cute clothing and footwear for kids can also be found. Semi-disgruntled employees serve you, but this doesn't seem to matter when a Calvin Klein underwear set is selling for less than $25. Other branches can be found Midtown on Madison Ave (212 557 4422), in the Financial District (212 422 4477), in Atlantic Terminal, Brooklyn (718 789 4477), and in Queens (718 760 7787).

Filene's Basement

4 Union Sq South, Upper West Side   212 358 0169

Filene's is the oldest off-price department store selling
a range of medium to high-end products to the urban
professional. The Union Square store is located above a DSW
shoe store, accessible through the building. Merchandise
rotates frequently with fresh truck deliveries arriving three
times a week. Designer jeans start from as low as $49.99,
while bridal gown sales see dresses originally priced at up to
$9,000 discounted drastically, then sold to the bevy of frantic
and sometimes tearful brides-to-be who camp out and rush
the store. Other stores are located in the Flatiron District (212
620 3100), on the Upper West Side (212 873 8000), and in
Queens (718 479 7711).

Henri Bendel

4 Union Sq South, Upper West Side   212 247 1100

Devoted to women (well, girls really), Henri Bendel caters to
the fashionably committed wealthy set (and their mothers).
Made up of two landmark buildings, the Rizzoli and the Coty,
it also has historic Lalique windows spanning the second to
fourth floors. The latest trends, reasonably and frighteningly
priced, mingle in a giant walk-in closet, while semi-annual
'Open See' events sees new designers showcase their
merchandise. There are no escalators, just elevators, and a
spiral staircase to ensure that no aspect of this picturesque
store is overlooked. The famed Federic Fekkai hair salon is on
the fourth floor.

Kmart

250 West 34th St, Midtown   212 760 1188

Made famous in the past for holding spontaneous 'blue light specials' and for the catchphrase 'attention Kmart shoppers,' this discounter allows you to buy big, even when your budget is small. Offering clothing, bedding, furniture, jewellery, beauty products, grocery products, electronics and housewares, you can justly furnish your apartment and not be ashamed to say that your curtains are made by Martha Stewart for Kmart. There is another Manhattan branch in the West Village (212 673 1540).

Macy's

151 West 34th St, Midtown   212 695 4400

Take two aspirin and prepare to be inundated with stimuli – Macy's is as famous for its annual Thanksgiving Day parade as it is for its endless sales. You can expect a full range of everything from inexpensive to designer for the whole family. Shops on the mezzanine level offer a reprieve from the crowds, where you can browse a wide hosiery selection or purchase something distinctive from the Metropolitan Museum of Art gift shop. A currency exchange counter is also located on the mezzanine. If you have a teenage daughter she will love the loud juniors department, or the icecream from the oddly placed Ben & Jerry's vendor. Macy's By Appointment is a complementary shopping service that can also ship items internationally. There is another branch on Fulton Street in Brooklyn (718 875 7200).

Saks Fifth Avenue

611 Fifth Ave, at 50th St, Midtown   212 753 4000

There are international locations of Saks in China, Saudi Arabia and Dubai, and in Midtown Manhattan, this shopping haven is a welcome retreat from Fifth Avenue. The store is considered the big sister to Bloomingdale's and pampers the sophisticated shopper who prefers to do damage in a quieter environment. The sixth and seventh floors are devoted to men, so women can drop them off and hit the designer shoe salons. Café SFA on the eighth floor delivers moderate fare and views of Rockefeller Center and St Patrick's Cathedral. Whether you go for the Elizabeth Arden Red Door Signature Facial at the spa, or visit the celebrated perfume department, you will always want to return.

Takashimaya

693 Fifth Ave, Midtown   212 350 0100

Great care has gone into making this Japanese store a calming haven for the avid shopper, which is evident in the level of quality and craftsmanship on display and the feeling of tranquility when you browse. Its mission statement is to combine Eastern philosophy with a Western practicality, and is reflected in the exquisite jewellery made by local and foreign artisans, men's and women's loungewear, tea shop, and floral boutique. World-renowned Santa Maria Novella skincare products and colognes are exclusively available here – the soap is reportedly the best in the world. The Home Collection on the third floor features unique tableware and lacquered chopsticks that make original gifts.

Markets

For those that prefer open-air shopping to pounding the department stores, New York has several markets to choose from.

For local produce, check out Essex Street Market (120 Essex Street btwn Delancy & Rivington Streets, www.essexstreetmarket.com, Mon to Sat, 08:00 to 18:00), which is 60 years old and especially great for wines and breads. The farmers' market at Union Square (held every day except Sunday and Tuesday) and Chelsea Market (75 Ninth Avenue, between 15th and 16th Streets, www.chelseamarket.com, Mon to Sat, 07:00 to 09:00; Sun 10:00 to 20:00), a city block full of gourmet food shops, as well as cosy cafes to stop off and refuel, are both choice destinations.

Grand Central Station has a bustling indoor market (www.grandcentralsquare.com) located at the east end of the main floor. The Garage (112 West 25th Street, between Sixth and Seventh Avenues, 212 647 0707) attracts fashionistas and designers to its flea market, where stalls simply overflow with vintage clothes, art and jewellery. Or, if you want a sprinkling of history with your haggling, the Malcolm Shabazz Harlem Market (52 West 116th St, between Malcolm X Blvd and Fifth Avenue, 212 987 8131, 10:00 to 17:00) is run by the neighbouring Malcolm Shabazz mosque, which houses the former pulpit of assassinated Muslim orator Malcolm X. The Harlem market offers African craft, such as tribal masks and drums, as well as bargain clothing, music and films.

Chelsea Market

Where To Go For

Books

Strand Book Store

828 Broadway at 12th Street, East Village   212 473 1452

You might need a ladder here, because Strand features towering stacks of books in every genre. Named in honour of an old literary magazine and the famous street in London, it has been a family business since 1927. The savings will definitely make you look twice, with up to 50% off hardcovers and paperbacks, and about 20% off 'front list' books. James Joyce's Ulysses may not be your idea of a holiday read, but this and other paperback classics start at $2.95. Dollar carts located outside make for good browsing, particularly if your tastes extend to the obscure. The peaceful third floor contains the city's largest rare book collection, where a first edition of Don DeLillo's Americana sells for $450. Strand has another location on Fulton Street (212 732 6070), as well as various 'street market' locations throughout the city.

Clothes

There's a reason so many New Yorkers are so well dressed – the city is possibly the best spot in the world for clothes shopping. Sure, Paris and Milan do a nice line in designer labels, but nothing can match the diversity that New York offers in terms of style, price and quality. The big department stores (p.170) are a good place to start, whether you prefer the fancy ones like Macy's, Bloomingdales and Barneys, or whether you're looking for fashion on the cheap at Century

21, Daffy's and Filene's Basement. But outside the department stores you'll find some pretty funky fashions: try Flying A (169 Spring Street, Soho, 212 965 9090) for urban brands and accessories, Scoop NYC (various locations, www.scoopnyc. com) for the latest styles in jeans, sweaters, dresses and prime label shoes, or Triple Five Soul (290 Lafayette Street, Soho, 212 431 2404) for competitively priced urban wear. Any fashionista worth her (or his) salt wears vintage clothing, and you'll find the best ranges of yesteryear's styles at Amarcord Vintage Fashion (252 Lafayette Street, Soho, 212 431 4161), Vintage by Stacey Lee (by appointment only, 914 328 0788), or Legacy (109 Thompson Street, Soho, 212 966 4827). And if your idea of fashion veers towards the dark side, you can find some great fetish and leather gear at The Leather Man (111 Christopher Street, West Village, 212 243 5339) and Purple Passion (211 West 20th Street, Chelsea, 212 807 0486).

If you still haven't found the perfect outfit, don't forget that Manhattan is home to countless branches of Gap, Urban Outfitters, Banana Republic, and many, many more.

Electronics

B&H

420 Ninth Avenue, Hell's Kitchen   212 444 6600

An extensive gallery of photo, video and audio equipment is housed in this superstore. B&H carries a remarkable range of stock, with in-store events showcasing new products from manufacturers. Digital cameras by Leica, Casio, Pentax,

Olympus, Rollei and Nikon, among others, can be purchased from $50 to $8,000. It also stocks studio, darkroom and lighting equipment, as well as a range of binoculars. Once you've selected your item just get a printout and head to the checkout where items appear as if by magic from the warehouse for you to take home (or get shipped, if you are short on suitcase space).

Home Furnishings and Accessories

If the plethora of homeware stores are anything to go by, New Yorkers must have some pretty stylish living spaces. Pottery Barn (www.potterybarn.com) and Crate & Barrel (www.crateandbarrel.com), both with multiple locations, are hard to miss, and stock funky home accessories, table ware and some nifty kitchen gadgets. For more unique items, try Fishs Eddy (889 Broadway at 19th Street, Flatiron District, 212 420 9020), where you will find kitsch, quirky dinnerware at reasonable prices – its Manhattan skyline crockery is hugely popular. And when looking for fashionable items for your home, don't forget those huge beacons of fashion – New York department stores. Macy's (p.176) and Bloomingdale's (p.172) both carry quality furniture ranges at prices that start out reasonable and then graduate to the overwhelming.

Top: Skyline crockery at Fish's Eddy, Bottom: Times Square

Jewellery

Tiffany & Co

727 Fifth Avenue, Midtown   212 755 8000

If you're shopping for jewellery in New York, Tiffany & Co should be at the very top of your list – women have been swooning over the contents of its little blue gift boxes since 1837. The jewellery is not off limits to anyone – the secret is in the silver, such as the $175 butterfly pendant by Elsa Peretti or Tiffany's own mesh ring for an obtainable $150. Internationally known and revered for its watches, diamond encrusted baubles, exquisite tableware and accessories, this stalwart also carries engagement rings that can bring both men and women to their knees. See serious shoppers discussing the four Cs of a diamond or witness young girls crowding the popular Tiffany & Co heart and logo chokers. Engraving is available, as is a complimentary personal shopping service. For those in need of a quick rest before the big spend, the sixth floor has restrooms and a lounge area.

Kids

FAO Schwarz

767 Fifth Avenue, Midtown   212 644 9400

In 1870, an immigrant from Germany named Frederick August Otto Schwarz opened a speciality toy store in lower Manhattan. With a keen eye for quality, innovation and fun, his store is now a 50,000 square foot menagerie of toys located in the landmark General Motors Building.

It is the oldest toy store in the US and is visited by wide-eyed children and adults alike. Barbie, Lego, plush toys, classic toys and games are just a few of the products to be found. The lower level focuses on baby through to pre-school products and sells items by Maclaren, Kate Spade and Neurosmith, among others. There is also a nursing area for mothers, which provides an escape from the main level, and houses an icecream parlour and bouncy kids high on sugar from the candy area. On the second floor, the 'dance-on piano' (featured in the famous 1988 movie *Big*) allows you to tap out Chopsticks after being taught by an instructor. Boys can construct cars in the Hot Wheels Factory, girls can make dolls in the Madame Alexander Doll Factory, and parents can pay prices that echo standard retail for toys and upwards.

Lingerie

Victoria's Secret
Various Locations

The Herald Square branch (212 356 8383) of this lingerie queen is part emporium and part disco. Cue infectious music, bright lights and men sitting on the sidelines as their significant others coo over lacy corsets, bow-adorned panties and ruffled bras. From the design collection, putter through creations by Dolce & Gabbana, Pleasure State and Andres Sarda, which are unique to this location and a few others. A Betsey Johnson pink floral slip can cost $58, while a French-inspired bra designed by Chantal Thomass can go for $108. The staff are experts, and will measure you for the best possible fit, then let you try on different bra shapes (plunge, wireless, demi, pushup, etc) before choosing your perfect bra from a huge range of beautiful styles. The beauty department carries makeup lines Pout, Vincent Longo, and Very Sexy (in case the atmosphere did not imply this enough), along with Victoria's body care and fragrance lines.

Souvenirs

You were probably bombarded with tiny Statue of Liberty pedestals, keychains, and T-shirts before you even left the airport. If you have managed to leave the terminal without a trinket, set your mind at ease, as there is plenty more where that came from. Tourist hotspots are usually crowded with souvenir shops. Step into Times Square and the sheer number of gift shops is almost more amazing than the neon signs. Some stores are standard in their offerings with the traditional phrase 'I love NY' emblazoned on many items. They sell ashtrays, snowglobes and sometimes even luggage in case you need an extra suitcase to take all your tack home. Canal Street, at the tip of Chinatown in downtown Manhattan, is another good option for souvenirs, as well as decent knockoff handbags for the ladies and watches for both him and her. Souvenirs are usually cheap, and for a couple of bucks, you can buy lasting memories. Of course, if you really want something that best represents New York with a slice of Americana, buy a pair of jeans. New York City is the foremost authority on denim.

Trinkets in Chinatown

Going Out

RADIO CITY
Music Hall RADIO CIT
PAUL SIMON SATURDAY OCTOBER 21 SOLD OUT

Introduction

Spend one night out on the buzzing streets of New York and you'll understand why it's called the city that never sleeps.

Few cities equal New York's world-class and marvellously diverse culinary offerings. Here in the foodie capital of America it's not so much a question of finding a cuisine, but rather choosing from the plethora of options when you do. The city boasts walnut-panelled French restaurants that rival those in Paris; boisterous Italian trattorias serving up robust sauces that hark back to grandma's kitchen in Naples; cacophonous Chinese banquet halls filled with the smoky tang of crackling peking duck; Middle Eastern mezze feasts of hummus and lamb kebabs followed by apple tobacco hookahs; and of course plenty of American comfort food, from gooey 'mac and cheese' to giant steaks and thick-cut french fries. As for costs, while New York has long been known (and often derided) for its $300 martini lunches and truffle hamburgers, in fact you can dine out – and well – no matter what your budget. Note that it's a good idea to make reservations, especially on the weekends, except for at the more basic, casual spots.

Once you're there, don't forget to tip. There is a sales tax of 8.625% which doesn't include service and given that tipping 15-20% is the standard, an easy way to calculate the amount is to double the tax. In the eyes of many, it's unacceptable not to tip as many in the service industry rely on the money to top up their salary.

Restaurants are generally open for breakfast from 07:00 or 08:00 to around 11:00, for lunch from about 11:30 to around 14:30 and for dinner from 17:30 onwards. The most popular time for dinner is generally from 18:30 to 20:00. Closing times vary: most restaurants serve food until at least 23:00, although increasingly you'll find many kitchens continue serving until midnight or shortly thereafter. And then there are the 24 hour eateries, which New York boasts plenty of – this is the city that never sleeps, after all. Most are diners, serving simple American fare like burgers and salads, and you'll find them across the five boroughs.

Drinking
As long as you are at least 21 years of age, alcohol flows freely in New York City. From cans of Pabst Blue Ribbon to high-end scotch, from potent shots to wine flights, and from $300+ bottles of champagne to exquisitely prepared speciality cocktails, bars cater to literally every taste and budget. In terms of drink prices, expect to pay $4-$7 average for a beer, $6-$12 for a glass of wine, and $8-$20 for a fancy cocktail. Soft drinks are usually around $2. For something even softer, unless you have a real aversion to tap water, it's worth giving New York's H20 a swallow – it's known for its quality taste (it's said that the city's famed bagels are so tasty because they're boiled in the local water). And, it is of course free, so you can save a pretty penny if you just tell your server, 'I'll have the New York water, please'.

Smoking

In July 2003, smoking in most New York businesses, including restaurants, bars, bowling alleys, dance clubs and pool halls, was banned and backed by hefty fines. Smoking is still permitted in 'cigar bars' (only cigars though – no cigarettes), personal cars, Indian casinos and private residences. Smoking has also been known to go on at certain 'members' bars' but the legality of this is hazy. The 'smoker's break' is now common NY practive, when the nicotine-addicted head outside of a bar or restaurant to get their fix – even in sub-zero temperatures.

Vegetarian Food

Vegetarians can dine well in New York. The city's well-known culinary creativity also applies to vegetarian restaurants, and many feature surprisingly imaginative menus. As is often the case, it's the neighbourhoods with a large student and youthful population that sprout the most veggie spots: Greenwich Village, the East Village and Soho feature a bevy of eateries. Increasingly, many of the city's restaurants offer vegetarian options on their regular menus – Daniel (p.231), for example, features a splendid vegetarian tasting menu. Indian, Middle Eastern and Kosher restaurants often feature largely vegetarian menus so stroll through Murray Hill, or 'Curry Hill', roughly around the 20s and 30s between Madison and Third Avenues, and you'll come upon a number of veggie-friendly eateries. If you're in the mood for some animal-free food, try Sacred Chow (p.248), Spring Street Natural (p.243) and Zen Palate (p.211).

Gay & Lesbian

Hipster bars, leather nightspots, throbbing dance clubs, fashionable restaurants – it's all here and terrifically queer. While gay hotspots exist in all five boroughs, the vast majority of fun awaits in Manhattan where you can easily stroll from venue to venue if you're in the right 'gaybourhood'.

Chelsea and Hell's Kitchen are prime hunting grounds, brimming with trendy establishments like Splash (p.203), that get busy with an after-work crowd and even hotter at the weekends. If you're looking for a scene that isn't so much of a, well, scene, then head to the East Village where you'll find a more low-key vibe along with guys whose primary focus isn't how much they can bench press. Or if you want to camp it up get over to Christopher Street in the West Village where the gay movement began with the 1969 riots outside the historic Stonewall Inn. Luckily, you don't need to fight for your right to party anymore in any of the street's flaming bars – the only struggle seems to be fitting into the tight shirts and trousers sold in the various colourful apparel shops in the area.

The Yellow Star

This pretty yellow star is our way of highlighting places that we think merit extra praise. It could be the atmosphere, the food, the cocktails, the music or the crowd – but whatever the reason, any review that you see with the star attached is somewhere that we think is a bit special.

Chelsea & The Meatpacking District

Home to some of the chicest restaurants and hottest clubs, celebs and open-minded party people flock to this 'gaybourhood' for a wild time.

Chelsea has an eclectic flavour – it has been the heart of the gay community for many years, and a magnet for artists, bohemians and free spirits. It is next door to the Meatpacking District – not long ago this was a wasteland of meatpacking plants and industrial buildings; now it is home to high-end shops, expensive clubs, and the luxurious Gansevoort Hotel.

Venue Finder

Top image: Bateaux New York

ENTREES

auteed red snapper with artichokes eks & basil oil	17
eamed mussel marinieres with pommes frites	15
ared atlantic salmon with fennel, weet peas & carrot sauce	16
pasted codfish with basil potato ree & yellow & red bell pepper sauce	16
e with couscous, portobello mushroom, ian capers & balsamic vinaigrette	15
oasted leg of lamb with eggplant, zucchini, peppers & puree of potato	16
ed cornish hen with herb risotto	15

Bateaux New York
Dinner Cruise

Pier 62, Chelsea Piers, West 23rd St
212 727 2789

The all-glass vessel means you won't miss a thing from the second you step on aboard. Choose from lunch cruises, afternoon sightseeing cruises, dinner cruises and themed cruises. Whatever your choice, you can enjoy gourmet cuisine, fine wine, a classic jazz soundtrack and fabulous skyline views. A dress code is enforced and jeans and trainers (sneakers) are an absolute no-no. Be sure to book well in advance to avoid disappointment.

Spirit Cruises
Dinner Cruise

Pier 62, Chelsea Piers, West 23rd St
212 727 7735

This luxurious boat and yacht group offers lunch, dinner and themed cruises and has two pick-up points; one in Manhattan and one in New Jersey. There seems to be something on all the time, be it DJ Jim Kerr's Love Boat Cruise or the Christian singles cruise. Check the website for a full list of events and prices, and be sure to book in advance.

One Little West Twelfth
Far Eastern

1 Little West 12th St
212 255 9717

The trendy One Little West Twelfth, with its exposed brick walls, high ceilings, flickering candles and top-shelf (and top-price) liquors, could be the poster child for the Meatpacking District. Come sunset, the beautiful people start piling in, eager to get buzzed on fusion cocktails while tasting their way through the global tapas menu of crunchy shrimp tempura and paper-thin slivers of Kobe beef, before hitting the clubs.

Ono at the Gansevoort Hotel (p.198)

Spice Market

403 West 13th St

Far Eastern

212 675 2322

Spice up your night at this sumptuous spot, helmed by celebrity restaurateurs Jean-Georges Vongerichten and Gray Kunz. In a city where space is at a premium, the 12,000 square-foot interior is particularly impressive. Try the grilled chicken with kumquats, mussels dunked in a lemongrass sauce and thick coconut sticky rice. If there's a wait – or even if there isn't – sample one of their potent and pricey Asian-accented cocktails.

Pastis

French
9 Ninth Ave   212 929 4844

Amid the velvet ropes of the Meatpacking District sits Keith McNally's Pastis, a lively bistro with aged mirrors and colourful, tiled floors, reasonably priced brasserie cuisine and a charged, flirty vibe. The classic fare includes a sliced steak sandwich topped with onions and gruyere cheese and a herb omelette with pommes frites. Wash it down with a hearty French red or two and then prepare to hit the nightclubs.

Ono

Japanese
Gansevoort Hotel, 18 Ninth Ave at 13th St   212 206 6766

Uber-hip restaurateur Jeffrey Chodorow's latest venture is everything you would expect; stylish Japanese fare in stunning surroundings. The multi-level interior flickers with lanterns, while windows offer views of bamboo gardens, where you can dine alfresco. Sip sake and sample the playful menu which boasts the chef's speciality of robatayaki; meats and vegetables grilled over an open flame, including skewered king crabs, scallops, clams, shiitake mushrooms, chicken livers and quail.

Gin Lane

Bar
355 West 14th St   212 691 0555

Paying $14 a pop for cocktails may sound hard to swallow, but the carefully crafted creations at Gin Lane go down surprisingly easy. Inside, singles mingle at the oak bar, while couples head to the romantic back dining area for steak, fancy salads, and gourmet macaroni and cheese. The sophisticated decor evokes speakeasies from eras past with chandeliers, mahogany walls, leather booths, Victorian wallpaper, and a well-dressed, formal wait staff.

Cain
Nightclub

544 West 27th St, Btn 10th & 11th Ave   212 947 8000

This safari-inspired nightspot is boasts servers in revealing khaki uniforms who bring pricey libations to a celeb-studded crowd. Exotic African decorative touches like zebra skin abound, while the natives get restless to the beats of the DJ, who spins from a boulder-like DJ booth. Cain's door is tough (buying a bottle helps), but once inside one feels like they're part of something special.

Marquee
Nightclub

289 Tenth Ave, Nr 26th St   646 473 0202

At the top of its game after three years in business – a lifetime in this town – Marquee's swanky bi-level, three-room space is still Plan A for most clubbers and celebrities. Enjoy a bottle in the hip downstairs Red Room, and dance to the hip hop-heavy grooves up front. A sweeping staircase is the club's focal point, but the people-watching is the real attraction – once you get past the doormen…

The Plumm
Nightclub

246 West 14th St   212 675 1567

A celeb favourite, this bi-level club features a bar on each floor and a tasteful decor of wooden walls, plants, inviting couches, artwork, and amber lighting; imagine a hip version of your living room. Once the location of legendary nightclub Nell's, celeb investors including Chris 'Mr Big' Noth have brethed new life into this address. Nightly events ensure a long line outside the (semi-strict) door, and the music flows from house to alternative to hip hop, rock, and 80s, with the beats varying on the two floors.

PM Lounge
Nightclub

50 Gansevoort St
212 255 6676

PM may be located in the hauter-than-hot industrial-chic Meatpacking District, but inside it's a Caribbean paradise of palm trees, high ceilings, bright colours, and coconut-scented air. The tropical theme makes its way to the menu as well, where dishes like coconut shrimp purses are washed down with pricey bottles of Patron Silver. If you'd like to enjoy island life, dress sharp and be prepared to splurge on bottle service.

Tenjune
Nightclub

26 Little West 12th St
646 624 2410

This celeb-filled hotspot shows no signs of slowing down (Beyonce, Joaquin Phoenix, and Penelope Cruz are just a few of the shoulders you may get to rub). Sip delicious libations like the Pure Chocolate at the sexy black bar, or take a seat on one of the velvet banquettes then follow the beats to the dance room with modern lounging areas. VIPs, meanwhile, can relax in a dark purple semi-private lounge complete with inviting fireplace. Naturally, a luxurious den like this is very exclusive, but it's worth it.

Food Bar
149 Eighth Ave

Gay & Lesbian
212 243 2020

This restaurant knows all the right ingredients to serve to its predominantly gay clientele; friendly locals, fun music and, of course, tasty dishes. Some tables are 'thisclose' to each other, so it's easy to mistake Food Bar for an actual bar. Then again, real bars usually don't offer such tempting dishes. But real restaurants don't usually have such an amazing bar. You'll just have to go there and solve this riddle yourself.

Gym Sportsbar
167 Eighth Ave

Gay & Lesbian
212 337 2439

This gym is worth visiting if you're eager to score home runs with some laid-back, jeans-and-T-shirt-type men. The big-screen televisions show all the big games but most patrons watch the tight ends in the bar. There's an outdoor terrace and a much-used pool table at the back – handy for making 'sticks and balls' innuendos. Every athlete needs to stay hydrated so don't miss $5 Svedka Tuesdays and $5 Absolut Thursdays.

Splash
50 West 17th St

Gay & Lesbian
212 691 0073

Splash is the kind of place where you'll create your own legends – it's all about having fun, from the hotties dancing under showers to the see-through bathroom doors. Check out their theme nights: frat-style parties on Thursdays, 'Full-Frontal' Fridays, and karaoke on Tuesdays keep Splash ahead of the gay party pack. And if that doesn't do it for you, the amazing happy hour (16:00 to 21:00) certainly will.

East Village

This arty part of town is a haven for food fans and those in need of a reviving pint of the strong stuff.

The East Village is a prime example of the gentrification that New York City is so famous for – a few short years ago, the area was run down, inexpensive, and fairly neglected. While it has always been a haven for artists, today the East Village is now a popular spot with and endless list of boutiques and tiny, yet oh so trendy, eateries serving food from many different countries.

Its proximity to NYU (and accompanying student population) makes the East Village a great nightlife destination. McSorleys (p.205) is a bit rough round the edges (not surprising, considering it's been there for over 150 years), but well worth a visit. If you're looking for something slightly more chic, enjoy a delicious meal in Prune (p.205) followed by a drink in the very vibey Bar Veloce (p.205).

Venue Finder

Bar Veloce	Bar	p.205
McSorley's	Bar	p.205
Mo Pitkin's House of Satisfaction	Bar	p.206
Nevada Smith's	Bar	p.206
Phoenix	Gay & Lesbian	p.206
Prune	American	p.205

Prune

American

54 East First St, Btn First & Second Ave   212 677 6221

A tempting pocket of country chic in the East Village, Prune warms the heart as much as it does the belly. Chef Gabrielle Hamilton's homegrown menu is nostalgic, with a twist, whether you sample the splendid brunch or the delightful diner menu that simple sizzles. Wooden tables, tiled floors and hand-picked flowers complete the snug scene – as do classic cocktails like Pimms Cup and Rose's Gimlett.

Bar Veloce

Bar

175 Second Ave, Btn 11th & 12th St   212 260 3200

You might need to suck in your stomach to fit into this very slim Italian wine bar, where a staggering selection of moderately priced vino and grappa is accompanied by small plates of panini and bruschetta. The dapper servers behind the brushed metal bar are extremely polished and professional. Ambient music plays, an old-school, European vibe pervades, and a chilled, 30-something crowd soaks it all in.

McSorley's

Bar

15 East 7th St   212 473 9148

Old, kind of cranky, and cheap: McSorley's Old Ale House is the grandpa of New York City bars. Established in 1854, and looking every day of it, this blast from the past should be on any visitor's to-do list, if only to take advantage of the $2.25 mugs of McSorley's Ale. Old newspapers line the walls, sawdust cakes the wooden floors, and and the chalkboard menu features a limited choice of snack food.

Mo Pitkin's House of Satisfaction

Bar

34 Ave A

212 777 5660

Only in New York, kids, only in New York. Take some Jewish heritage, throw in a dash of down-home comfort food, add a pinch of Latin flair, and stir in an exuberant helping of comedy, live music, and performance art, and the result is Mo Pitkin's House of Satisfaction. Diners wash down Jewish and Latin-inspired dishes like the Cuban Reuben, potato latkes, and deep-fried mac 'n' cheese with He'brew beers and cocktails like Mo's Famous Orange Julius. Everything comes with a side of kitsch.

Nevada Smith's

Bar

74 Third Ave, Btn 11th & 12th

212 982 2591

When Nevada Smith's says it's where 'football is religion', they're talking about soccer, and it comes in the form of the English Premier League and other European matches that are broadcast live – even if that means opening the bar early in the mornings. Naturally this spacious wooden den welcomes a lot of (mostly male) homesick expatriates, and the fact that Guinness, Carlsberg, and Boddingtons are all on tap is the icing on the cake.

Phoenix

Gay & Lesbian

447 East 13th St

212 477 9979

You'd think you were in a straight Upper East Side bar rather than a gay East Village one after stepping into this place. Surrounded by a plain, nondescript decor, with beer in hand and wearing baseball caps, the patrons here are some of the straightest gay boys you'll find. But rest assured, your favorite Cher song will come on the jukebox in no time. A low-key vibe is matched by low-priced drinks, from $1 Buds on Wednesdays to $2 domestic beers on Sundays. A pinball machine, video games, and a pool table help draw in a decent number of patrons during the week.

Gramercy Park & Flatiron District

From bed-bound happy hours to NYC's best hot chocolate, this neighbourhood will delight the senses and blow your mind.

Gramercy Park has a tangible air of exclusivity, particularly when it comes to its beautiful park, to which only those that live in the townhouses along its border have a key. However, you don't need a key to enjoy the rooftop bar at the Gramercy Park Hotel (p.37), which has breathtaking views and killer cocktails. The Flatiron District is named after the iconic triangular-shaped building at 23rd Street where Fifth Avenue intersects Broadway. Despite being largely a business area, in the evenings when all the suits have gone, there's a thriving nightlife that is perhaps slightly more upmarket than other, more bustling areas further south.

Venue Finder

Zen Palate (p.211)

Old Town Bar & Restaurant
45 East 18th St

American

212 529 6732

Old-world New York doesn't get much better than this: a tin ceiling, dark booths and a crowd of crusty regulars, college jocks and trendsters jostling for space at the long bar. The kitchen turns out juicy burgers, crispy onion rings, tangy BBQ wings and giant salads which you can wash down with a frothy beer or two into the wee hours.

Union Square Cafe
21 East 16th St

American

212 243 4020

The perennial success of Danny Meyer's Union Square Cafe hinges on a simple concept: contemporary Italian-influenced American fare made with the freshest local ingredients. You'll find everything from a classic, juicy burger to a poppy-seed bun to semolina dumplings with baby potatoes and pesto cream and polenta infused with gorgonzola. The wine list features excellent California vintages. For a sweet finale, dig into the berry pie.

Tocqueville
1 East 15th St

French

212 647 1515

From the flickering candles on the linen-covered tables to the thick carpeting and plush chairs, Tocqueville is a parfait blend of French romance and class. The seasonal menu abounds with market-fresh entrees, like chilled green and white asparagus drizzled in black truffle vinaigrette and seared scallops with artichokes, forest mushrooms and fava beans and one look at the dessert list is enough to kill any diet.

Casa Mono
Spanish

52 Irving Place, Btn 17th & 18th St   212 253 2773

The menu may be adventurous, but the ambience is rustic
Spain, with an open kitchen and tables set close together.
Croquettes are flavoured with pumpkin and goat's cheese
while the patatas bravas are liberally spiced with onions and
cayenne pepper. Seafood lovers are also spoiled for choice: try
mussels steamed in sparkling cava, squid, dorada (sea bream)
and salted cod.

Zen Palate
Vegetarian

34 East Union Sq, Btn 15th & 16th St   212 614 9345

Zen Palate doles out veggie specialities with a kick, like
eggplant and bok choy in a spicy garlic sauce, sweet yam fries,
scallion pancakes and Shredded Heaven, a heaping plate of
chives, bean sprouts, three kinds of shredded soy, taro spring
rolls and brown rice. Wooden screens and wicker chairs offer
an earthy backdrop while the crowds keep it lively. The other
branch is on Ninth Avenue (212 582 1669).

71 Irving Pl.
Cafe

71 Irving Place   212 995 5252

Clusters of small round tables fill the front of the room (there
are also two outdoor tables), which boasts a cocoon-like
vibe thanks to exposed brick and dim lighting. A coffee bar
in the rear of the space serves up a lengthy menu that runs
the gamut from coffee ($1.48 for a small) and coffee floats to
beer and wine. Sandwiches, panini, homemade waffles, and
pastries are all on offer.

City Bakery
Cafe

3 West 18th St, Union Square
212 366 1414

Two words: hot chocolate. It's exquisite and the kicker is the enormous square marshmallow that accompanies it. An area at the back boasts fruit and yogurt and salad bars, although everything from couscous to catfish can be found. A large island in the middle of the space is where customers pay, order their drinks, and ogle baked goods like croissants, cookies, and tarts.

Flatiron Lounge
Bar

37 West 19th St
212 727 7741

A black cocktail dress-clad hostess greets you at the mirrored entrance of this retro-chic den, where soft lighting, cool piped-in jazz, and a womb-like arched pathway leading to the bar signal a sophisticated evening ahead. Cocktails like the $12 Martinez and New York Sour are paramount here, and the well-heeled, older-skewing crowd knows better than to order a beer (though it's available, at $7-$11).

Duvet Restaurant and Lounge
Nightclub

45 West 21st St
212 989 2121

Mattresses take centre stage at this Flatiron restaurant and lounge. A Monday-Friday happy hour gives Duvet an after-work scene, with diners staking claim on the welcoming beige and gold beds to feast on steak tartar rolls and pork tenderloin. Things get livelier as the evening progresses, with the house-y music growing in intensity. The unisex downstairs bathroom is also a must-see!

Flatiron Lounge

Financial District

Beneath the monoliths of money and around the world's most profitable street, traders and tourists can choose to eat and drink in spots ranging from the tacky to the trendy.

The Financial District buzzes with the energy of thousands of suited stockbrokers and well-heeled power players. Although the 9/11 attacks were a tragedy for all of New York, it was this area that felt it the most – it lost one of its most famous landmarks and many of the people who worked here every day. However, it didn't take long for the Financial District to bounce back and today it is as bustling as ever.

In terms of nightlife, you'll find plenty of suits enjoying an after-work cocktail, but it's not exactly the area to be in if you're looking for a 24 hour party. However, there are some interesting spots to hang out in – the Fraunces Tavern (p.215) is an essential stop off if you're interested in the history of the country – it's been serving food and drink since 1762 and one of its early customers was George Washington himself. Killarney Rose (180 Beaver Street at Pearl Street, 212 422 1486) is a classic Irish bar – it may not have the history of Fraunces Tavern, but the *craic* is good.

Venue Finder

SouthWest NY
American
225 Liberty St, 2 World Financial Ctr   212 945 0538

When Wall Streeters are in need of some south-of-the-border escapism – and potent shots of tequila – they sprawl out on SouthWest NY's ample waterfront deck and feast on cheesy quesadillas, tasty lobster clubs and hefty burgers. On the weekends locals come to kick back and soak in the rays and the liquor.

Spice Grill
Indian
18 Murray St   212 791 3511

The dishes here are a refreshing departure from typical Indian fare: the fried Banarsi Samosa, for example, is crammed with potatoes, crumbled feta cheese and tangy pomegranate seeds, while the naan is enhanced with pesto. Shrimp are tossed in a delicate sauce of basil and coconut milk. Convenient for Wall Street and downtown, Spice Grill draws a lively lunch crowd, although business slows down considerably come nightfall when all the suits head home.

Fraunces Tavern
Bar
54 Pearl St   212 968 1776

George Washington may not have been able to tell a lie, but he had no qualms about enjoying a pint at this historic watering hole, which dates back to 1762. Today, it's captains of industry and Wall Street dealers who frequent this colonial relic, sealing deals over lunches of beef wellington and rack of lamb in the quaint dining room. If you've got an appetite, go for the New York strip steak and chicken with a garlic glaze.

Lower East Side & Chinatown

Peking duck and raucous rock make these areas your best bet for budget boozing, delicious dim sum, or a nice cup of tea…

The Lower East Side used to be considered one of the seedier parts of town, although it is becoming more popular all the time, with many artists, writers and professionals having moved into the area. The LES nightlife is legendary – head for Clinton or Ludlow Streets (between Rivington and Stanton) and you'll find some excellent live music venues, including the Bowery Ballroom (www.boweryballroom.com).

Chinatown has grown in leaps and bounds over the last few decades, and of course this is where you go when you've got a craving for genuine Chinese food – you can't go wrong with Jing Fong (212 602 9988) or Ping's Seafood (p.217).

Venue Finder

wd~50
American
50 Clinton St
212 477 2900

wd~50 embodies New American cuisine. Chef Willie Dufresne pairs seemingly disparate ingredients to create magical dishes: mediterranean bass is served with artichokes, cocoa nibs and brittle peanut; a pinenut cassoulet envelops rabbit sausage and smoked octopus; and a rack of lamb is flavoured with banana consomme and served with broccoli and black olives. At $105, the nine-course tasting menu is not a bad deal.

Ping's Seafood
Chinese
22 Mott St
212 602 9988

Settle in with a hot tea at this spirited Chinatown favourite, and before long deft waiters are whisking out fish so fresh it's practically flopping on your plate. Chef and owner Chung Ping Hui wisely eschews any fancy preparation and the seafood is lightly steamed and served with simple sauces, such as garlic-ginger. The decor is typical Chinatown but Ping's is the real deal.

Katz's Deli
Deli
205 East Houston St, at Ludlow St
212 254 2246

This renowned Jewish deli offers up pastrami towering on rye, layers upon layers of hot corned beef slathered with mustard and steaming, giant knoblewurst – garlic beef sausage. The famous 'I'll have what she's having' scene in *When Harry Met Sally* was filmed here – a hanging sign marks the spot. For dessert, try an egg cream, a uniquely New York concoction of milk, chocolate syrup and carbonated water.

Clinton St. Baking Co.
4 Clinton St

Cafe
646 602 6263

In the mood for buttermilk biscuits, blueberry pancakes, and a steaming-hot cup of cafe con leche? Unfortunately, so is everyone else, as evidenced by the crowds waiting outside. But good things come to those who wait: dishes like the crab cake sandwich and Southern breakfast are winners, and drinks like hot apple cider and Harney & Sons' passion plum tea are a nice way to wash it down.

Teany
90 Rivington St

Cafe
212 475 9190

Opened in 2002 by musician Moby with his former girlfriend Kelly Tisdale, this teahouse and cafe now has its own cookbook, a line of refrigerated flavoured tea beverages and tea accessories, and a Teany To Go takeout space. While there are 98 teas to choose from, most people are drawn to Teany's reasonably priced baked goods and vegan and vegetarian items like the incredible goat's cheese and artichoke salad.

Arlene's Grocery
95 Stanton St

Bar
212 995 1652

Downtown rock bars come and go but Arlene's Grocery is still going strong after more than a decade. The cover's cheap and bands play nightly. It's best known for its insanely popular Monday night Rock and Roll Karaoke, where aspiring rockers can screech their lungs out to their favorite Guns N' Roses and Led Zeppelin hits while backed by a live band. On Sunday nights Kuntry Karaoke takes over.

Mercury Lounge   Bar
217 East Houston St   212 260 4700

Any indie band worth its salt has played this live music venue. This is a musicians' rock club, but the fans are happy campers too thanks to low ticket prices and excellent acoustics. A front bar hosts the pre-show crowd, and Mercury Lounge claims to have a tombstone embedded in its bar countertop. Fortunately, the only things haunting the club are the ghosts of the rock legends who've played here.

Welcome to the Johnsons   Bar
123 Rivington St   212 420 9911

Two words: cheap beer. In a city of $14 martinis, it's comforting to know that there are still places where one can find three beers for $10. This divey den boasts little more than a jukebox, a pool table, and two scary, but functioning, bathrooms, but that and the cheap shots are all the motivation the laid-back crowd needs.

Element   Nightclub
225 East Houston St   212 254 2200

The massive former bank greets clubbers with a long line and an intimidating door, but inside it's an all-out dance party. A more intimate downstairs space is well-suited to private parties, while the top floor has a VIP space overlooking the main dancefloor. This club oozes energy, and it's all dictated by whatever DJ happens to be on the decks. Saturday night's Bank party is especially popular.

Midtown & Hell's Kitchen

Home to some of the best clubs in town, not to mention Restaurant Row where you can find affordable and diverse cuisine.

With Times Square, the Empire State Building, Grand Central Station, a large chunk of Fifth Avenue and some of the city's largest department stores within its borders, the Midtown area is busy, busy, busy. And wherever you find crowds, you're sure to find hundreds of food and beverage outlets to serve them – this is certainly the case in Midtown, where you can eat your way around the world without straying too far from your hotel.

Venue Finder

Carl's Steaks

American

507 Third Ave, At 34th St

212 696 5336

Skip the drive to Philly – this Murray Hill favourite serves up the juiciest cheesesteaks in New York. Owner Carl Provenzano knows his cheesesteaks; made with sliced or chopped beef, melted cheese and grilled onions and served with perfect Italian rolls, they deliver on all counts and, most importantly, have won the endorsement of native Philadelphians. The cheese fries and chili are also crowd pleasers.

District

American

130 West 46 St

212 485 2999

With a Broadway-esque decor of spotlights and woven steel curtains, District is one of the new wave of good theatre district restaurants. The menu caters to the theatre crowd, with a 'short pour' of select wines to accompany your pre-show meal. They even offer goodie bags to nibble on during the show. Afterwards, stop by and play critic over an espresso and cheesecake or apple cobbler.

Norma's

American

118 W 57th St, Btn Sixth & Seventh Ave

212 708 7460

For the ultimate brunch, head to the classy Norma's in Le Parker Meridien Hotel, where you can feast on dishes such as the house eggs benedict served with a buttermilk pancake layered in bacon and the rock lobster and asparagus omelette. For sweeter options, go for the chocolate French toast, heaped with strawberries and pistachios, or lemony griddle cakes topped with thick Devonshire cream.

Carnegie Deli
Deli

854 Seventh Ave, At 55th St
212 757 2245

This quintessential New York deli has it all: monster sandwiches, joke-cracking staff, celebrity headshots on the 'wall of fame', sour pickles on every table and a line out the door, especially at lunch. Size matters here: some sandwiches weigh a whopping three pounds, teetering on the plate, daring you to eat the whole thing. But don't miss the creamy cheesecake, among the best in NYC.

Le Cirque
European

One Beacon Court, 151 East 58th St
212 644 0202

Few restaurants capture New York's joie de vivre – and ego – like the lavish Le Cirque, which reopened amid much fanfare in 2006. Owned by the savvy, gregarious Sirio Maccioni, this latest incarnation boasts a dazzling blend of haute decor and cuisine that draws plenty of famous faces. The Italian-French food, when it comes, seems almost like an afterthought – but it's as bold and flavourful as the rest of the place.

Opia
European

130 East 57th St
212 688 3939

Striking the perfect balance between haute and hip, the plush Opia brings some welcome zing to Midtown's dining scene with Mediterranean flair. The main lounge and bar is an inviting spot to chill out over a cocktail or lunch by the floor-to-ceiling windows. For a more formal meal, head to the second-floor dining room. They also do a good weekend brunch and show all Champions League football matches at the bar.

DB Bistro Moderne

55 West 44th St

French

212 391 2400

For foodies on a budget, this bistro offers the renowned cuisine of Daniel Boulud at lower prices than at his signature Daniel (p.231). In the spacious dining room, where traditional European decor meets modern Manhattan, the menu offers classic dishes, fine-tuned for the American palate. Try the famous DB burger stuffed with foie gras and truffles. It's the most expensive in NYC – but you definitely won't forget it!

The Modern

Museum of Modern Art

French

212 333 1220

When MoMA reopened in 2004, it wasn't just its Picassos and Van Goghs that had everyone salivating – it was also the food. The Modern's exquisite contemporary French fare includes pork tenderloin marinated in wheat beer with barley risotto and turnips, juicy beef poached in an earthy cabernet, chorizo-crusted cod, as well as over 900 vintage wines and a sommelier to guide you through the list.

Triomphe

49 West 44th St

French

212 453 4233

The lovely, understated restaurant Triomphe serves up simply prepared French fare like seared filet mignon with creamed spinach and ricotta gnocchi, and plump chicken breast drizzled in a cranberry puree with warm bread dumplings. Though small, Triomphe makes the most of the space it has, with an elegant dining room and is the ideal place for a date, either before or after the theatre. One of Midtown's best-kept secrets.

Grand Central Oyster Bar
Grand Central Stn, 42nd St

Seafood
212 490 6650

The Grand Central Oyster Bar opened in 1913 when Grand Central Station first started operating, and is located in its gorgeous vaulted underground. They serve up oysters prepared in every way imaginable – but best slurped down raw, sprinkled simply with lemon juice. Alternatively, try the fresh salmon, sea bass, trout or swordfish. Accompanying the food is an impressive wine list from around the world.

AVA Lounge
210 West 55th St

Bar
212 956 7020

Modern-day hepcats can gaze out at Times Square and the Hudson River from this stylish penthouse lounge at the Dream Hotel. Named after Ava Gardner, the bar's soft colours and mod furnishings fittingly capture a Rat Pack ambience. In the summer, the outdoor space transforms into a lush English garden where Manhattan's movers and shakers sip martinis as they take in the stunning view.

Latitude
783 Eighth Ave

Bar
212 245 3034

If bigger is better, then this massive bar and lounge is the cream of the crop. Top 40 tunes blare, sports are broadcast on TVs, and an after-work crowd make themselves at home on the three roomy floors, including a swanky upstairs lounge and a casual downstairs dining space. Drink specials make it easy on the wallet, and the menu runs the gamut from Buffalo wings to coconut shrimp.

AVA Lounge

The Grand

Nightclub
41 East 58th St   212 308 9455

Grand indeed. This opulent nightclub has brought new
energy to an area better known for department stores than its
nightlife. Through a translucent wall is a yellow-walled nook
where partiers recline on velvet settees in this James Bond-
reminiscent lounge, or dance to the DJs spinning mainstream
and hip hop hits. The clientele is a more down-to-earth, young
professional crowd than at the super-trendy downtown clubs.

Noho, Nolita & Little Italy

Get a slice of the action along with your pizza. Bistros, bars, boutiques and beer – what more could you ask for?

Once one of the largest Italian neighbourhoods on the east coast, Little Italy has now shrunk to just a few blocks of Italian restaurants and street vendors. Still, it's a great place to experience some of the Italian culture, or at least the food. The neighbourhood still celebrates the feast of San Gennaro for 11 days each September. The street closes to vehicular traffic and pedestrians are free to stroll from one food vendor to another, sampling the sausage and peppers, calzones, pastas and tiramisu while listening to live music and street entertainment. Just norrth of Little Italy is the tiny area of Nolita, best known as a boutique shopping destination. It is also home to some excellent restaurants, many of which are Italian.

Venue Finder

Il Buco

Il Buco

European

47 Bond St, Btn Lafayette & Bowery 212 533 1932

Il Buco is possibly the most rustic retreat you'll find in the city, with wooden floorboards, copper pots hanging from the ceiling, and a range of market produce on display. The food is masterful, with a selection of seasonal Mediterranean appetisers and main courses such as tuna crusted in wild fennel pollen, pan-fried king prawns in a sea-salt crust, and even the miraculously simple plate of olives marinated in fennel flowers and rosemary (you can almost taste the sunshine).

Café Gitane
International

242 Mott St, Btn Prince & Houston St
212 334 9552

A petite slice of French Morocco in the heart of Nolita, Café Gitane's itty-bitty outdoor cocktail tables are 'parfait' for channelling your inner European and ogling the passing trendsters. Tuck into nibbles, like spicy olives and tart oranges or a terrific combo of gorgonzola, walnut and honey, and wash it all down with a French red or an imported beer.

Lombardi's
Italian

32 Spring St, Btn Mulberry & Mott St
212 941 7994

For over 100 years, this Little Italy landmark has been serving up some of the best pizza in New York. It's all about the crust – baked in a coal-fired oven, it emerges perfectly charred on the outside and warm and doughy on the inside. The justly famous clam pie is topped with clams, romano cheese and black pepper. While some recent renovations have left parts of Lombardi's interior a bit antiseptic, there are still enough original nooks that recall the good old days.

Agozar
Latin American

324 Bowery St, At Bleecker St
212 677 6773

An island atmosphere pervades at Agozar, in decor and in spirit. The lively entrance that opens onto Bowery Street gives way to green palms fronting bright yellow walls, and come dusk, becomes a hotbed for flirting. The dinner plates are whisked off, the tables are pushed together and dancing – plus more imbibing – is heartily encouraged until about 01:00 or later, depending on how many are left standing.

Cafe Angelique

68 Bleecker St

Cafes & Coffee Shops
212 475 3500

Cafe Angelique charms with its provincial French country cafe vibe. Cafe tables pepper the sidewalk, and the interior is cosy. An impressive selection of hearty soups, gourmet sandwiches, salads, pastries, and breakfast dishes like a mushroom omelette sandwich are on offer and the quaint farmhouse atmosphere and ambient music are ideal.

La Esquina

106 Kenmare St

Bar
646 613 7100

An air of intrigue permeates this glam grotto, which features dark lighting, candelabras, dungeon-like railings, and a bar area where puddles of candle wax line the counter. Couples and small groups pack the tiny tables (reservations are a must), and a wayward elbow could land in a neighbour's ceviche. Tequila connoisseurs will marvel at the outstanding selection, which pairs nicely with the seafood specialities.

Butter

415 Lafayette St, Btn East 4th St & Astor Pl

Nightclubs
212 253 2828

Celebrities regularly make appearances at this downtown hotspot, whether it's to nibble on high-end American cuisine in the vaulted-ceiling dining room (check out the gorgeous birch forest mural), sip a speciality cocktail at the bar, or groove downstairs in the lounge where a DJ spins and the pretty people perch on cedar seats. Butter's greatest asset is its warm wood decor which unfortunately gets lost during the busy weekend period.

Upper East Side & Central Park

Elegance abounds on 'Millionaire Mile' so shine those shoes, get ready to flex the credit card and spot some celebs.

The Upper East Side is home to some of the most expensive real estate in the US. It also has the nation's highest concentration of individual wealth – in other words, there's a lot of rich people living here, and it shows in the restaurants you'll find in the area. You can expect to find plenty of the city's finest French restaurants (usually with a celebrity chef at the helm), serving up delicious delicacies at a price. Blend in by donning your twinset and pearls and partaking in a posh afternoon tea at the Rotunda inside the Pierre hotel (p.233), or enjoy a dignified dinner at Aureole (p.231). It's not all posh though – you can still enjoy a down-to-earth, all-you-can-eat, raucous night at Brother Jimmy's (p.233).

Venue Finder

Aureole	American	p.231
Brother Jimmy's	Bar	p.233
Café Boulud	French	p.231
Daniel	French	p.231
Harry Cipriani	Italian	p.232
KAI Restaurant	Cafe	p.232
Ship of Fools	Bar	p.233
The Rotunda at The Pierre	Afternoon Tea	p.233
Uptown Lounge	International	p.232

Aureole
American
34 East 61st St   212 319 1660

The elegant, hushed Aureole, awash in romantic details from
fresh flowers to ornate silver cutlery, has become the ultimate
'special occasion' restaurant. Revered chef Charlie Palmer's
daring culinary style emerges in every dish, from delectable
thyme-scented veal sweetbreads with cepes to monkfish
braised in persimmon and lobster salad drizzled in a ginger
vinaigrette, with the added kick of wasabi.

Café Boulud
French
20 East 76th St, Btn Fifth & Madison Ave   212 772 2600

The younger, but no less impressive, sibling to Daniel, Café
Boulud offers up the same exquisite French fare – at more
affordable prices – in an intimate dining room awash in earthy
hues. Burnished mahogany-lined walls and cream curtains
give way to rich brown banquettes and carved dark-wood
chairs. The talented team of chefs delight the palate with four
different menus: seasonal, global, traditional and vegetarian.

Daniel
French
60 East 65th St   212 288 0033

Daniel's regal dining room sets the tone for the feast to
follow: pillars rise to lofty ceilings amid an Italian Renaissance
decor of mosaics, detailed moldings and plush red chairs.
Daniel Boulud and his team wows the palate with a menu
that showcases every season of the year. If you'd like to soak
up the luxurious atmosphere without breaking the bank,
head to the adjoining bar and lounge for exotic cocktails.

Uptown Lounge

International

1576 Third Ave, At 88th St   212 828 1388

The stylish Uptown Lounge, with a skylight bar and circular booths, hums nightly with a glossy crowd. The lively speciality nights include Sangria Sundays, with $6 pitchers, and Tuesday Jazz nights. The global menu offers up Thai chicken skewers, nachos topped with grilled chicken, fried calamari and coconut shrimp. If you'd like a more substantial meal, feast on the grilled steak or duck breast in plum sauce.

Harry Cipriani

Italian

781 5th Ave, Btn 59th & 60th St   212 753 5566

Even in a city saturated with swank celebrity hotspots, Harry Cipriani gleams like a well-cut diamond. Smitten celebs, the moneyed set and anybody who thinks they're somebody flock here nightly to tuck into northern Italian fare – such as calamari risotto – and sip sweet bellinis. For all the stars that strut in and out, the interior is refreshingly casual, with mustard walls, hardwood floors and a welcoming bar.

KAI Restaurant

Cafe

822 Madison Ave   212 988 7111

This sleek, pristine restaurant and teahouse is perched above the immaculate ITO EN shop, which sells the Japanese brand's line of teas and accessories. Come in for the afternoon tea service, where fragrant brews are paired with delicate Japanese pastries. The dark-wood space exudes a calming Zen atmosphere, and the usual menu, while limited to a handful of sushi and omakase dishes, is of the highest quality.

The Rotunda at The Pierre
The Pierre Hotel, Fifth Ave at 61st St

Afternoon Tea
212 838 8000

This grand lounge features some of the most distinctive trompe l'oiel murals you'll ever see. The light tea includes scones and a choice of finger sandwiches or cakes, while the full tea has all of these piled up on high on a three-tiered silver tray. If you really feel like indulging, have the Royal Tea, which includes a glass of sparkling wine or port

Brother Jimmy's
1485 Second Ave

Bar
212 288 0999

Anyone who thinks Manhattan bars are all about expensive cocktails, snobby doormen, and ear-assaulting house music obviously hasn't been to Brother Jimmy's. The rustic decor could best be described as 'trailer park after a tornado' chic, with checkered tablecloths, beer signs, and lots of pigs. A Southern Appreciation Day on Wednesdays gives a 25% food discount to patrons with a valid Southern ID.

Ship of Fools
1590 Second Ave

Bar
212 570 2651

If it involves a ball, whether kicked, hit or dribbled,, the 40 plus TVs at Ship of Fools will be airing it. Welcome to the sports headquarters of Manhattan. During the football season, Ship of Fools has more guys wearing jerseys than the Super Bowl and stomach-lining staples like mozzarella sticks and burgers, and unbeatable drink specials, which range from $4 margaritas and $2 pints during the week to the $30 wings and beer bucket deal.

Upper West Side

Romance the one you love or meet your own Carrie or Mr Big in some of the finest establishments in the city.

This is one of the most famous areas in the city, if not the world. Every time you have watched a movie or TV show featuring scenes of Central Park, with its beautiful greenery bordered by some of the most luxurious apartment buildings you can imagine, you are looking at the Upper West Side. Some of the city's most famous restaurants are found in the area, including Jean Georges (p.235) and Tavern on the Green (p.235). The area is well known for its brilliant brunch offerings – the perfect way to refuel after a long walk in the park. Barney Greengrass (451 Amsterdam Avenue at 86th Street, 212 724 4707) is one of the best, and you should expect to wait for at least an hour before you get a table. For a classic New York hotdog that is rumoured to be a favourite of Lauren Bacall, head to Gray's Papaya at the corner of 71st Street and Broadway.

Venue Finder

Bin 71	Bars	p.236
Cafe Lalo	Cafe	p.236
Jean Georges	French	p.235
Penang	Far Eastern	p.235
Shalel Lounge	Bar	p.236
Tavern on the Green	American	p.235

Tavern on the Green
American

Central Park, at West 67th St
212 873 3200

The contemporary American cuisine (grilled salmon, juicy steaks, salads and the like) is rather pricey for what you get, but then that's not really the draw. Rather, it's the chance to experience a New York icon. If you're on a budget, go for the Garden Bar menu (service starts at 17:00), with tasty appetisers like grilled chicken quesadilla heaped with avocado or a crispy bruschetta, for around $9–12.

Penang
Far Eastern

240 Columbus Ave, at 71st St
212 769 8889

Penang's fusion cuisine has struck a fine balance with its Malay and Pan Asian dishes. The champ of appetisers is the Roti Canai, a crispy Indian pancake with curry chicken dipping sauce. Vegetarians can indulge as freely as meat-eaters; and for dessert, how can you pass up pancake stuffed with ground peanuts?

Jean Georges
French

Trump International Hotel
212 299 3900

The sleek interior, with soaring windows overlooking Central Park, is the perfect backdrop for the phenomenal French dishes, which epitomise chef Jean Georges Vongerichten's philosophy in the kitchen. He keeps it refreshingly simple – meats and fish are often cooked whole and on the bone while introducing vibrant new flavours, many of which have emerged from his experiments with wild edible plants including nettles, chickweed and garlic mustard.

Cafe Lalo

201 West 83rd St

Cafe

212 496 6031

The spacious but very crowded brick-and-tile interior boasts floor-to-ceiling windows and vintage French posters. Attractive waitresses in tank tops run back and forth with orders, and upbeat European pop music plays, creating a somewhat frenzied atmosphere. Cafe Lalo is a picturesque, whimsical spot for dessert, espresso, or wine – they're open until 04:00 on Friday and Saturday and until 02:00 the rest of the week.

Bin 71

237 Columbus Ave

Bar

212 362 5446

This cosy, dimly lit wine bar oozes with maturity, and that's not just a reference to the aged wines it serves. An older, intellectual crowd clusters around the petite room's few small tables, nibbling on crostini, panini, and desserts as they savour their glasses of reds and whites. Jazzy tunes add to the elegant scene. A wonderful setting for a romantic date.

Shalel Lounge

65 West 70th St

Bar

212 873 2300

If romance doesn't ignite at Shalel Lounge, it clearly wasn't meant to be. Shalel's dark Moroccan-inspired grottos create a fantasy world thanks to global beats and exotic fixtures like hanging lanterns, curtains, a trickling stone fountain in the back, mirrors, floor pillows, and knick-knacks from faraway lands. The long bar serves a respectable list of beers, wines, and somewhat pricey speciality cocktails, along with dishes like couscous.

Clockwise from top: Cosmopolitans, Jean Georges (p.233)

Tribeca & Soho

Utilitarian warehouses and industrial alleys have given way to glamorous nightspots filled with beautiful people.

Tribeca is a neat snapshot of New York gentrification, with Robert DeNiro championing its rebirth into an area of urban chic. Both Tribeca and Soho are famous for their gothic architecture, cobble-stoned streets, fabulous shopping and great restaurants. A cutting edge art scene and sumptuous shopping are matched by the quality and variety of restaurants, bars and cafes of this popular area.

Venue Finder

Clockwise from top left: Balthazar (p.242), Bubby's Pie Company (p.240), Kittichai (p.240)

Bubby's Pie Company

American

120 Hudson St, at North Moore St   212 219 0666

At Bubby's, you can fill up on American favourites like 'mac and cheese', buttermilk fried chicken and meatloaf and gravy in homely surroundings. The challenge here is in choosing your pie – selections include sour cherry, banana cream, chocolate peanut butter and the mile-high apple pie. These are all made from scratch using recipes culled from kitchens throughout the Midwest and Brooklyn. Bubby's is, not surprisingly, a hit with youngsters, with a creative and nicely priced kid's menu.

TribeCa Grill

American

375 Greenwich St, at Franklin St   212 941 3900

Robert DeNiro has done much to put Tribeca on the map. Thanks to his efforts, it has become one of the hippest enclaves in the city. He opened the TribeCa Grill with restaurateur Drew Nieporent in 1990 and this modern restaurant has been a roaring success ever since. The grilled meats and seafood are rivalled only by the people-watching, and you may spot anyone from Uma Thurman to DeNiro himself.

Kittichai

Far Eastern

60 Thompson St   212 219 2000

The owners here know their trendy Soho demographic well. The fusion Thai would go unrecognised in its native country, but Kittichai's delectable, inventive cuisine – along with its orchid-strewn, Asian-inspired interior – has earned it heaps of well-deserved accolades. The menu skews towards Thai

Woo Lae Oak

'tapas' so you can try the wide array of sweet, sour, and spicy concoctions. The staff all look like models, but they're also consummate professionals, guiding you knowledgeably through the menu.

Woo Lae Oak
Far Eastern
148 Mercer St, Btn Prince & Houston St   212 925 8200

Woo Lae Oak's menu has the same dishes as its no-nonsense Koreatown cousins, but the sleek decor is pure Soho. So are the clientele, who often pop in after a day of shopping to relax over martinis and potent fruity cocktails while digging in to Bi Bim Bop (cold veggies over rice) and Dae Ji (grilled pork). You can also barbecue your black tiger prawns, tuna loins, filet mignon or sliced beef tongue over the grills embedded in the tables.

Balthazar
French
80 Spring St, Btn Broadway & Crosby St   212 965 1785

New Yorkers adore Balthazar, and on any night you'll see well-heeled, cocktail-clutching revellers laughing it up, either at the candle-topped tables, around the bar or spilling out onto Spring Street. New York's answer to a Paris brasserie, it serves up splendid spreads, no matter what time of day. Brunch brings forth poached eggs and smoked salmon, while for dinner you can tuck into steak frite and sauteed black cod.

Bouley
French
120 W Broadway, Btn Duane & Reade St   212 964 2525

Bouley is regularly rated as one of New York's finest restaurants. The French-American cuisine is a testament to Daniel Bouley's training at the Sorbonne in Paris and some of the best restaurants in Europe and the US. The dishes are presented with a flourish and the service is among the finest in the city. You feel graciously cared for from the moment you step in to the low-lit, elegant dining rooms.

Fiamma Osteria
Italian
206 Spring St, Btn Sullivan St & Sixth Ave   212 653 0100

The glass elevator at Fiamma travels all of three floors, but still, ascending in hushed comfort to the dining room lends a certain cachet to the evening – as do the attentive staff, who are knowledgeable about the nuovo Italian cuisine on offer. It's also a spot known for its tasty cocktails and impressive wine list and you can enjoy your buzz in the lovely lounge, which is done up in inviting reds and oranges, with flickering candles.

Blue Ribbon Sushi
119 Sullivan St

Japanese
212 343 0404

Manhattan's many sushi lovers rate Blue Ribbon highly, which explains the long wait on many nights. Stick it out, though, and a fresh, flavourful sushi feast is your reward. If you'd like to watch the slick sushi chefs in action, take a seat at the bar at the front. Otherwise, retreat to the romantic back room, where you can suckle fresh fish and sake surrounded by a stylish Soho crowd doing the same.

Nobu
105 Hudson St, At Franklin St

Japanese
212 219 0500

Getting a reservation at Nobu can be tricky, but what sweet victory when you do. Latino and European influences are apparent in the black cod and miso, mussels livened up with salsa and yellowtail sashimi topped with jalapenos. The place is a celeb magnet, so you'll no doubt spot plenty of recognisable faces amid the decor of stone walls and birch trees.

Spring Street Natural
62 Spring St, at Lafayette St

Vegetarian
212 966 0290

This Soho stalwart, blessed with a prime corner perch at Spring and Lafayette, is among the finest vegetarian restaurants in New York. The wide-ranging menu has something for anyone craving organic, healthful fare, whether they are vegetarian or not. For under $10, you can feast on a breakfast special of eggs with chicken apple sausages, oven-roasted potatoes and organic coffee, or stuffed sandwiches like almond veggie burger with white cheddar on a sesame bun.

Brandy Library Lounge
Bar

25 North Moore St
212 226 5545

Welcome to the best library ever. Okay, so there aren't that many books, but the shelves are stacked with almost every brandy, whiskey, and rum known to man. Jazz plays in the upscale lounge, as local business folk settle into their leather chairs and sample steak tartare and exquisite single-malt scotch. The bar also hosts frequent tastings and a 'spirit school,' which explores a different spirit at each lesson.

Pravda
Bar

281 Lafayette St
212 226 4696

Prolific restaurateur Keith McNally is behind this Russian caviar bar and vodka lounge, but it's more fun to pretend that this is a secret KGB hideaway. Given the hush-hush vibe and Iron-Curtain-chic metal tables, it's not hard to do. Frosty thoughts of the Cold War are banished by the stylish subterranean bar's ambient lights and the belly-warming vodka martinis, which come in flavours as diverse as coconut, sake, and pear.

Vino Vino
Bar

211 West Broadway, at Franklin St
212 925 8510

Rustic exposed brick walls and sleek leather couches host oenophiles who come to sip 20 plus wines by the glass, experiment with a wine flight, and nibble on cheese plates and cured meats. Free champagne and wine tastings occur weekly, and frequent live jazz and bossa nova performances create intimate and sophisticated warmth. The wine shop carries over 200 labels, so you can buy a bottle to enjoy at home.

Canal Room

Nightclub

285 West Broadway, at Canal St   212 941 8100

Part swanky downtown spot, part cheap music joint, Canal Room is an interesting hybrid. The lineup of performers varies from reggae to folk to tribute bands to 80s one-hit-wonders, with cover charges rarely rising above $20. The concert space is large but retains intimacy, with a bar to one side where fans can grab a beer and an empanada. When a band's not playing, the space becomes a nightclub, complete with DJs, modern furniture, and a glass-enclosed VIP room.

West Village

You'll recognise this area from the big screen, but the food and fun on offer will be a whole new experience.

These are some of the most desirable spots in the city – the quiet tree-lined streets frame the cosy brownstones, which are just blocks away from some of the best nightlife in New York. Once known as a refuge for musicians and artists, the village is now a melting pot, with people from every walk of life living, working or playing here.

Venue Finder

49 Grove	Nightclub	p.252
Alta	Spanish	p.248
Babbo	Italian	p.247
Back Fence	Bar	p.251
Corner Bistro	American	p.247
Da Silvano	Italian	p.247
Dean & Deluca	Cafe	p.250
Doma Cafe & Gallery	Cafe	p.250
Dove	Bar	p.251
Down the Hatch	Bar	p.251
Employees Only	Bar	p.250
Grey Dog Coffee	Cafe	p.252
Sacred Chow	Vegetarian	p.248
Sushi Samba 7	Latin American	p.248
The Duplex	Gay & Lesbian	p.253
Dirty Disco	Night Club	p.252

Corner Bistro
331 West 4th St

American
212 242 9502

Ask any local where to find the best burger in NYC and chances
are they'll direct you here and tell you how cheap it is. For four
bucks you can sink your teeth into a juicy meaty eight-ouncer.
While the bar itself is nothing to write home about it's the
burgers you come for. You may find a queue at the weekend
when the bar comes in pretty handy for a few cold ones.

Babbo
110 Waverly Place

Italian
212 777 0303

This acclaimed restaurant sits paces from Washington Square
Park, and not too far from Little Italy, but the cuisine is a
pleasant surprise. It's all about simplicity and freshness; dishes
are based on seasonal produce, and the finest seafood, meat
and game. Highlights include the mint love letters with spicy
lamb sausage, succulent rabbit with red cabbage, and the
spicy two-minute calamari.

Da Silvano
260 Sixth Ave

Italian
212 982 2343

Believe the hype: Da Silvano offers Cucina Toscana as tasty
as the beautiful eye-candy crowd that struts in every night.
Larger-than-life owner Silvano Marchetto presides over
his cosy, eclectically furnished restaurant with panache.
The robust, earthy Tuscan fare includes Silvano's famous
panzanella, bread pudding seasoned with sea salt and tangy
red vinegar; juicy pepper tuna steaks; mussels dunked in
garlic, olive oil and white wine; and all kinds of pastas.

Sushi Samba 7
87 Seventh Ave

Latin American
2126 917 885

After appearing in an episode of *Sex and the City*, fusion hotspot Sushi Samba 7 became a de rigueur destination for show groupies. Crowds flock here for the loungey vibe, tropical cocktails and 'Latinese' cuisine of fresh ceviche, grilled shrimp and sushi rolls with salmon, tuna and other fresh fish. In summer, revellers take to the roof garden, sipping fruity drinks under the stars. There's a Brazilian brunch at the weekends.

Alta
64 West 10th St, at Sixth Ave

Spanish
212 505 7777

Alta takes a lofty approach to Spanish tapas, or 'little plates', and the result has New York's gourmands gushing. The impish creations whisked out from the bustling kitchen include peekytoe crab enveloped in white polenta, fried goat cheese squiggled with lavender-infused honey, and lamb meatballs studded with dates and pine nuts. As for wine, the choice is clear: try one of Spain's earthy Riojan reds.

Sacred Chow
227 Sullivan St

Vegetarian
212 337 0863

Vegetarian joint Sacred Chow's cheeky logo – a meditating cow with thick eyelashes – and cheery red walls set the stage for the fare here: playful dishes such as tapas of tofu in sunflower pesto and hefty soy meatballs; the jaw-stretching Hot Diggity Soy Dog; and Italian frittata, a tofu omelette with vegan mozzarella. Wash it down with a delicious Very Berry or Gym Body (bananas, toasted almonds, cinnamon and soy milk) smoothie.

Clockwise from top left: Dean & Deluca (p.250), Down the Hatch (p.252), Sushi Samba 7

Dean & Deluca
Cafe
75 University Pl
212 473 1908

In this branch of this minimalist-but-hip chain, urbanites from textbook-toting students to paper-reading senior citizens jockey for space around a horseshoe-shaped table. The sparse, all-white room also holds several small tables and a counter where laptops are put to good use. An adjacent room serves up lemon bars, bagel sandwiches and coffee.

Doma Cafe & Gallery
Cafe
17 Perry St
212 929 4339

A sense of community pervades this open space of white exposed brick, tasteful art, and wall-length windows. Customers can grab a book off the shelf to read while they sip their coffee or wine, and people often leave their newspaper behind for someone else to enjoy. Even patrons' furry friends are looked after, with dog bowls left outside by the sidewalk benches. The extensive menu includes pate and artichoke sandwiches.

Grey Dog Coffee
Cafe
33 Carmine St
212 462 0041

Country-style cafe Grey Dog, with its red exterior and assortment of paintings of dogs (what else?), sees a predominantly late 20s crowd line up for fresh coffee and hot cider. A menu above the counter is written in coloured chalk and includes comfort food gems like pancakes, banana bread and matzoh ball soup, in addition to gourmet salads and sandwiches, while a jazz soundtrack keeps things mellow. Flickering candlelight provides a romantic vibe at night.

Back Fence
Bar
155 Bleecker St   212 475 9221

Although today Greenwich Village teems with more tourists than Beat poets and musicians, it's still worth paying homage to the area's creative history by checking out the singer-songwriters and bands that play at the Black Fence. This no-frills joint hosts two to three musicians per night, and there's open poetry readings on Sunday afternoons. Leave expectations and pretensions at the door.

Dove
Bar
228 Thompson St   212 254 1435

With its red velvet-flocked wallpaper, roaring fireplace, and intimate candlelit seating, Dove teems with the sexy vibe of a retro speakeasy. A glance at the cocktail menu reveals old-fashioned indulgences like sidecars, grasshoppers, and french lavender martinis. The vibe picks up as the evening progresses, with Billie Holiday tunes giving way to The Smiths. Dove does not serve food.

Employees Only
Bar
510 Hudson St, Btn Christopher & West St   212 242 3021

This old-school wedge of the Village got a welcome shot in the arm with the arrival of this stylish speakeasy-style bar and restaurant. The slick crew behind the venture were once employees at some of Manhattan's trendiest spots, and they've managed to create an ambience that's both timeless and very 'now'. You'll feel cooler by the second as you sip on a $12 Pimm's Cup or Pisco Sour cocktail.

49 Grove
49 Grove St

Nightclub

212 727 1100

This intimate subterranean lounge is a chic purplish-blue lair of velvet couches. The club is no stranger to celebrity sightings – there's a VIP room and a fleet of luxury vehicles available for the well heeled. Hip hop, funk and house encourage dancing, but it's hard for the trendy crowd to resist the lure of kicking back with a cocktail in the stylish surroundings.

Dirty Disco
Btn Seventh & Eigth Ave

Nightclub

212 206 9600

Dirty Disco brings the dancing minus the drama. Working its hip but not snobby crowd into a frenzy with 80s, rock, and hip hop tunes on the petite dancefloor, the bi-level club is known for its powerful sound system and 70s-disco-inspired decorating scheme of disco balls, funky wallpaper, sleek low banquettes, and black and white photos of naked women. Surprisingly, it all comes off as stylish, not cheesy.

Down the Hatch
179 West 4th Street

Bar

212 627 9747

When it comes to sports, beer, and raunchy good times, nobody does it better than Down the Hatch. In this underground alpha-male den the game is always on, the Atomic wings are always hot, and the foosball, darts and beer pong competitions are always in progress. It's the epitome of a lowbrow hangout, but sometimes a little bit of a rowdy drinking experience is just what you need.

49 Grove

The Duplex

61 Christopher St   212 255 5438

Punters belt out their favourite show tunes at this friendly gay
& lesbian West Village piano bar. Open mic starts at 21:00, so
you've got plenty of time to work up some Dutch courage.
If singing is not your thing, it's great fun to watch those who
slur off-key. The cabaret room often hosts some real talent,
in case your ears need a break, and there's a games room if
you're just not feeling musical. But perhaps one of the best
features about the Duplex is its terrace overlooking the West
Village's cruisiest intersection.

Entertainment

Get plenty of rest before you visit New York: you'll need to save your energy to make the most of the nightlife. From theatre and cinema to cabaret and the thriving comedy scene, there's rarely a dull moment in the city that never sleeps.

Cabaret & Strip Shows

Things can get steamy in this city. For the most part, it's pretty much harmless fun: a $20 lap dance here, a few gyrating topless dancers there. What's not so harmless is the cost: between the cover, pricey drinks, tips, and 'special services', customers drop dollars as quickly as the dancers drop their clothes. In-your-face sex is so passe, but neo-Burlesque has taken the city by storm and continues to titillate without cliche. The clothes come off slower, the sultry moves are white-hot, and the scene is fuelling a burlesque revival in the city. The Va Va Voom Room at Fez (212 579 5100), is a weekly neck-craning riot and touted as New York's best, with tickets starting at $15, with a two drink minimum.

Casinos

The only gambling done in New York City is deciding whether or not to risk using a dive bar's bathroom. But if blackjack is calling your name, Atlantic City, New Jersey is just a two-and-a-half-hour Greyhound bus ride away, and bus passengers are even given a cash-back bonus to gamble with when they arrive at the casino. You must be over 21 to gamble; that's partly due to the free cocktails that are given to gamblers. The new Borgata Hotel Casino & Spa (www.theborgata.com) is easily the flashiest of all the casinos, and even has swanky nightclubs and fine restaurants under its roof.

Cinemas

New York – a city that has starred in scores of movies – is a boon for film fans. Movie theatres run the gamut from the glittering Ziegfeld (212 307 1862), an old-world theatre that seats over a thousand, to multiplex palaces with stadium seating, monster screens and super expensive gourmet snack bars. Tickets hit the $10 mark a while back, and the average price is about $11, with some posh spots charging up to $13. Matinees (generally before 16:00) are $3–4 dollars less, as are tickets for seniors and children. New York also boasts a well-oiled indie and foreign film scene, with several venerable movie houses, such as the Angelika (Soho, 212 995 2000) and the Film Forum (West Village, 212 727 8110), dedicated to showing independent and global flicks. The prestigious New York Film Festival has been running for nearly half a century, and showcases new films from around the world. The Tribeca Film Festival, spearheaded by Robert DeNiro to revitalise Manhattan after the 9/11 attacks, features a huge range of new films, musical concerts, street fairs and film lectures.

Comedy

This is one city that takes comedy seriously. Though the jokes themselves can be hit or miss, the variety of talent that

New York City offers is unparalleled. Because performers and showtimes can vary widely, it's best to contact comedy clubs directly to see what's on the schedule. Note that a cover charge and drink minimum is almost always in effect but there's no drink minimum at Upright Citizens Brigade (307 W. 26th Street, 212 366 9176, www.ucbtheatre.com) or Comix (353 W. 14th Street, 212 524 2500, www.comixny.com).

One definite must-visit is Harlem's Apollo Theater (212 531 5300, www.apollotheater.com), famous for its amateur night, where nervous stand-up wannabes face heckling from the crowd. The venue has also hosted musical greats such as Ella Fitzgerald, Billie Holiday, Sammy Davis Jnr, James Brown – the list is endless. Many an artist has claimed their fame after an appearance at the Apollo which still has a massive fan base, whether for its historical significance, its cultural legacy, its architectural importance or just its guaranteed good nights out.

Concerts

Live music is a huge part of the New York City scene. Mega-bands like U2 and the Rolling Stones have played to sold-out crowds at Madison Square Garden, while more alternative and up-and-coming bands play more intimate venues like Irving Plaza and Bowery Ballroom. The Blue Note (131 West 3rd Street, 212 475 8592), Birdland (315 West 44th Street, bt Eighth and Ninth Avenue, 212 581 3080), and Dizzy's Club Coca-Cola (Time Warner Center, Columbus Circle, 212 258 9595) are popular jazz haunts, while Lincoln Center is home to the esteemed New York Philharmonic. Come summer, festivals like Central Park SummerStage

The Blue Note

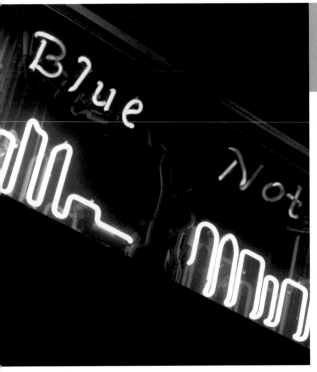

(www.summerstage.org), Siren Music Festival (www.villagevoice.com/siren), and Celebrate Brooklyn (www.celebratebrooklyn.org) offer free concerts.

Theatre

One word: Broadway. The Great White Way is home to some of the world's finest theatrical productions, from musicals like *Les Miserables* to dramas like the recent *History Boys*. Theatres are clustered around Times Square, with performances generally running Tuesday through Sunday, with matinees on Wednesday and Sunday. Expect to pay anywhere from $60–$110 for a decent seat, although purchasing tickets via www.playbill.com or waiting on line at the TKTS booth in Times Square (www.tdf.org/tkts) can fetch better deals on select shows. Strangely, the later you book your tickets, the cheaper they can be – so if you have a free evening ahead it may be worth paying TKTS a visit in the late afternoon. Off-Broadway and Off-Off-Broadway shows are less expensive and often offer more avant-garde alternatives. Visit www.nytheatre.com for updated show listings.

> ### Hot Tip for Tickets
> There is a lesser-known alternative to the TKTS booth in Times Square, where the queues are usually much shorter. Head for the corner of Front and John Streets at South Street Seaport (you can take the M15 bus all the way down Second Avenue). See www.tdf.org/tkts for more info on opening times.

Clockwise from top left: Radio City Music Hall, Jazz in Central Park, Times Square

History in the Making

The 'discovery' of New York was an accident (twice!). The first jolly wanderer was Giovanni de Verrazzano, an Italian commissioned by the French to find the Orient. Instead, he sailed straight into the harbour in 1524 and named it New Angloueme, after the French King Francis I. As soon as he realised his error, Verrazzano turned right around, never officially setting foot on the land. It wasn't until 85 years later that British explorer, Henry Hudson, commissioned by the Dutch this time and also in search of the elusive Orient, stumbled into the Hudson River (yes, he named it after himself), proclaimed New Angloueme for the Dutch and renamed it New Amsterdam.

The indigenous Lenape tribe had lived in what is now New York for thousands of years, farming the land and living in relative comfort in a lush and unspoiled habitat right up until the Europeans stumbled across it.

By 1613 the Dutch Fur Settlement was established, and the Dutch West India Company sent over 100 settlers to the southern tip of the Island (Mannahatta). The Lenape tribe defended their land and only conceded defeat after several

Sculpture of Rockefeller Center construction workers

courageous battles. In 1626 Peter Minuit, the first governor of New Amsterdam, decided to try a different tack with the locals and pulled off the city's first real estate scam by persuading the tribe to trade all of Manhattan and Staten Island for goods valued at the historical equivalent of $500.

The British have always been keen to get in on the act with new settlements, and with things suddenly looking up in New Amsterdam, they wanted the whole pie, not just a piece. In 1664 they swooped in and got the lot. The government didn't put up any kind of fight, unlike the Lenape (yep, still around) who fought some pretty ruthless battles. Thousands died, and those that survived were forced upstate. European settlers now numbered 3,000 and the city got a new British name: New York (after the Duke of York, who was the brother of King Charles II).

Inevitably, citizens were less than happy with the pomp and taxes introduced by the British and the American Revolution took place between 1775 and 1783. New York started its battle against the Red Coats on 26 August 1776 and after seven bloody years, two major fires and thousands of lives lost, George Washington and his men marched victoriously down Broadway, reclaiming the city. On 13 September 1788 New York became the first capital of the Red Coat-free United States of America. Less than a year later, on 30 April 1789, General George Washington was inaugurated as the first president in the Federal Hall Building on Wall Street. New York remained the capital city until 1790 when the honour was bestowed to Philadelphia.

Immigrants were coming in by the boatload, factories were chugging, poverty was rife and the crisp, costly clothes of the rich upper set were being stained with the muck of the ordinary. Reluctant to give up aesthetics to house more immigrants, and inspired by the grand green open spaces of London and Paris, the Central Park Commission set up a design competition in 1853. The result: America's very first landscaped park. The winners, designer Federick Law Olmstead and architect Calvert Vaux, took the next four years to produce the lush Central Park, which stretched two and a half miles long and half a mile wide.

Being a city based entirely on immigration and a hodgepodge of ethnicities and nationalities, New York tension was on the brink of eruption and in 1863 it finally exploded in one of the city's ugliest battles ever, the Draft Riots. All men were forced to fight in the civil war, unless of course

New York Stock Exchange

they could cough up the $300 exemption fee. This meant that the wealthy stayed safe and the poorest of the poor, predominantly the huge Irish community, were forced to take arms in a battle they wanted nothing to do with. On 13th July, an Irish mob of 15,000 took to the streets in bloody protest leaving a whirlwind of damage in their wake. They destroyed shops, homes, and then the riot took an even more ugly turn. Blaming the black community for the civil unrest (the American Civil War was fought for many reasons, superficially with the intention of freeing the black slaves) and fearing free slaves would mean stealing work from the white workforce, the mob turned against people of colour, vandalising their homes, burning down the Colored Orphan Asylum and even beating and lynching black people in the streets. Four days and 105 deaths later, peace was finally restored.

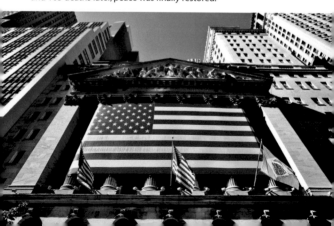

By 1898 the population of New York had boomed to over three million, and the city limits had spread well beyond those laid out in the previous century. The five boroughs (the Bronx, Manhattan, Staten Island, Brooklyn and Queens) were brought together officially to make up New York City.

The height of European migration came in the 1920s, as thousands upon thousands came to America seeking a better, more prosperous life. Streaming through the processing centre on Ellis Island port, their first encounter with the new world would be the breathtaking sight of the Statue of Liberty and all that she stood for. Between 1892 and 1954, an estimated 15 million immigrants flowed through the harbour, prodded through the processing office, through health checks, inspections, interrogations and examinations. It is said that some 40% of all Americans have an ancestor that arrived at Ellis Island. Some moved on to pastures new, others (as many as five million) stayed in the sprawling metropolis.

The Statue of Liberty, originally called 'Liberty Enlightening the World', was a gift from the French to mark America's 100 years of independence from the British. Shipped in parts and assembled in New York, Lady Liberty had no base on which to stand. Money for her pedestal was raised by the affluent Hungarian immigrant and publishing mogul, Joseph Pulitzer (publisher of The World daily newspaper), who encouraged Americans to dip into their pockets. And dip they did, finally unveiling the copper beauty in 1886. The Statue of Liberty is the tallest statue in the world, standing a clear 305 feet high on her base, which is an 11 pointed star.

Statue of Liberty

By the end of the century land was fast becoming a rare commodity but the flow of people was not ebbing in the least. The race to grow upwards (instead of outwards) was on and by 1902 the city was able to boast a whopping 66 skyscrapers. And then came the growth below. In 1900 the underground transit system (or more commonly, the subway) tagged a $35 million spend and moved thousands of New Yorkers around the five boroughs less than a decade later.

They say that when New York sneezes the rest of the country gets a cold. On Tuesday 29th October 1929, the city gave an almighty 'atchoo' as the stock market crashed and the country plummeted into what came to be known as The Great Depression. Adding insult to injury, the corrupt dealings of Mayor James J Walker finally caught up with him and then the rest of the city as one million New Yorkers lost their jobs. It wasn't until tough talking, Jewish-Italian Fiorello LaGuardia (nicknamed 'the little flower') took office after Walker resigned (1932) that the place took a turn for the more prosperous. The Great Depression had hit hard and president Herbert Hoover found himself in one almighty bind. Americans blamed Hoover's passivity and felt that his initiatives to help were too late and too lame. New York native Franklin D. Roosevelt, next in line and 32nd president to the batting post, was ready for some radical experimentation in order to get the country out of the dark pit it currently found itself wallowing in. The New Deal was struck up. Some programmes worked and some didn't, but the country slowly crawled out of the depression and started on its bid to be one of the greatest economies of the world.

New York hurtled through the 20th century truly making the era its own. The art scene boomed as young hip things moved into the village (east and west) to make it home to all things bohemian. Andy Warhol and The Factory (his studio and its army of hangers-on) moved all things contemporary to the city, as he did with his protege, Brooklyn born Jean-Michel Basquiat. Everyone who was anyone would mingle at The Factory, from Mick Jagger and Salvador Dali to Bob Dylan and Allen Ginsberg. The literati were everywhere. Legendary club CBGB opened in the village and the music scene was the icing on the city's cake, with the likes of Bob Dylan and Joan Baez hanging around. Then came Woodstock, the sexual revolution, a proud gay community and everything in between. New York was the place to be, it was party central, intellectual haven, rock hangout and just downright cool!

On 11 September 2001 New York faced one of its most fatal tragedies, as terrorist attacks destroyed the twin towers of the World Trade Center. That day, thousands of lives were lost and the entire nation was rocked to its foundation. The American economy was shattered, as was its 'you-can't-touch-us' resolve.

The world mourned as the entire country came to a complete standstill and New York fell to its knees. The 'war on terror' began and Afghanistan and Iraq felt the physical blows. New York and its inhabitants have since recovered, licking their wounds as the foundations for the new Freedom Tower are set in place to stand on the ruins of what was. The rest of the world however, is still reeling from the day that never should have happened.

New York Timeline

1524   Giovanni de Verrazzano sails into New York, renames it after a French king and sails right back out

1613   The Dutch Fur Settlement was established, and the Dutch West India Company sends over 100 settlers to try and fill the place. City renamed New Amsterdam

1626   First governor, Peter Minuit, trades land with the indigenous tribe, the Lenape

1664   The British take over and rename it New York

1783   George Washington reclaims New York

1788   New York becomes the first capital of the United States of America

1789   George Washington inaugurated first president in the Federal Hall Building on Wall Street

1853   Work on Central Park begins

1863   The Draft Riots ravage the city

1883   Construction of the Brooklyn Bridge is completed (after 13 years)

1886   The Statue of Liberty is unveiled

1898   The Bronx, Manhattan, Staten Island, Brooklyn and Queens are joined to form New York City

1892	An estimated 15 million immigrants stream through Ellis Island
1904	The New York City Subway opens
1929	New York stock market crashes and the Great Depression begins
1931	Empire State Building is officially opened
1934	Fiorello La Guardia takes over as Mayor from the corrupt James J. Walker (resigned 1932)
1946	New York becomes the official home of the United Nations
1952	UN Headquarters is built
1969	The Woodstock Music Festival takes place in Bethel, New York. 500,000 people attend
1977	The New York City Blackout lasts for two days and the subsequent riots and looting mark a lowpoint in New York's history
1980	John Lennon is murdered in front of his apartment near Central Park
2001	Terrorist attacks destroy the twin towers of the World Trade Center
2011	Freedom Tower is due to open in the place where the Trade Center towers stood

New York Today

Today New York is one of the world's most powerful cities. It is an undisputed leader in terms of business, fashion, arts and entertainment, and attracts nearly 50 million visitors each year.

New York has always been home to some of the country's finest, and most forward thinking, minds and the 21st century is no different. The city's liberal (and often anti-Bush) standpoint makes it a truly unique and refreshing destination within America, with hip young things, culture vultures and just about everyone else flocking to the metropolis every year to see what the fuss about.

All tourists are welcome in New York, regardless of nationality or travel budget, and official figures report over 43 million people paid the city a visit in 2006 – with 7.2 million coming from overseas. This popularity places a real strain on resources but with 70,000 hotel rooms currently available and another 5,000 to be added in the next year, New York is, as ever, rising to the challenge.

The reasons to visit New York are endless, and unless you are staying for months, you probably won't get to do everything in one visit. The many parades held throughout the year are the ultimate excuses to party - wear silly hats and drink green beer (on St Patrick's Day, when New York is second only to Ireland itself in terms of celebration). Or revel in the (chilly) streets on Thanksgiving, accompanied by giant

cartoon characters for the annual Macy's Thanksgiving Day Parade. New York also hosts various film and fashion festivals throughout the year, and these are worth marking on your travel calendar. While the catwalks of New York Fashion Week are for invited industry professionals and VIPs only, the vibe is tangible everywhere and the city is full of celebrities.

One of the most popular tourist destinations is the site where the World Trade Center Towers once stood before that unforgettable day in 2001 (see p.51 for more information). Even if you are not American it is hard not to be moved by the incredibly poignant display of photographs taken on the day and the days afterwards, when ordinary New Yorkers made heroic efforts to find the missing, comfort the grieving, and heal the city.

There remains a buoyant, if defiant, air on the streets in the years since 9/11 and you'll see reminders of this tragic day in unexpected places. The centre of this energy is focused at Ground Zero, where the Freedom Tower is due to open in 2011. This 1,776 foot skyscraper will sit where the World Trader Center twin towers once stood in downtown Manhattan and will feature office space, a rooftop restaurant and an observation deck. There will also be a memorial and museum at the site which are said to reflect 'absence' – the two designers are aiming for two voids to represent the 'footprints' of the twin towers, with an oak forest including cascading water falling into an illuminated reflecting pool. For the time being, the site is a cross between a giant construction yard and a very moving tribute to those who lost their lives.

This was never a city to rest on its laurels though and

developments are popping up all over the five boroughs. You can even see all the action from the new observation deck on the top floor of the Empire State Building which opened in 2006 to celebrate the 75th birthday of the iconic landmark. The views are the same, if a little higher, than those from the traditional deck on the 86th floor but the extra space should ease some of the queues for this tourist favourite.

By 2008 one thing you might be able to spot on a very clear day (don't hold your breath) is the High Line Park in the Meatpacking District. What was once a bustling railway 30 foot above street level is now being transformed into 'the nation's first urban water park' with 26 acres of wave pools, waterslides and an indoor beach club.

Fans of more traditional water-side pursuits should visit the ever-popular Coney Island on Brooklyn's south shore which is getting a long overdue nip/tuck job. For a mere $83 million the shoreline, with its creaking rollercoaster and famed hotdogs from Nathan's, will be turned into a year-round entertainment destination.

The museum scene will also get a new lease of life in the coming year: some old (the National Cartoon Museum, formerly the International Museum of Cartoon Art, gets a new home), some new (the first ever sports museum will open in Spring 2008 in lower Manhattan) and some just because they can (the lower east side will welcome a new art museum, the first ever in the Downtown area). With a city like New York, it just gets bigger and better all the time so you'd better find your new favourite restaurant and start planning your next trip.

Tradition & Culture

This buzzing metropolis is a vibrant, intoxicating magnet for anyone and everyone. From street vendors to world-class entertainment, new music to art movements, it's easy to see why New York is the capital of cool.

The Ultimate Melting Pot

New York is a celebration of culture – everyone's culture! It doesn't matter where you came from, once you step foot in the Apple, the only thing that matters is making a part of it yours. The fact that this is everybody's home makes the city one of the most culturally rich and ethnically abundant in the world.

This is home to some of the world's cultural elite, from the Algonquin Round Table (humble beginnings of the renowned New Yorker magazine) to icons like Truman Capote, Jackson Pollock, Allen Ginsberg, John Lennon and Herman Melville – all have gravitated around the Big Apple and helped shape the global art scene.

The city's liberal attitude towards ethnic blending and acceptance of the unorthodox make it a fertile ground for creativity. Art galleries, museums, theatre and film are all here in an abundant tribute to all things cultural.

From its earliest days, the city has attracted an eclectic mix of people and has a larger range of ethnicities than almost anywhere else. Race relations in the city have twisted and turned along a turbulent timeline. However, considering the number

of different cultures living together on one tiny island (and the boroughs), it's a relatively perfect example of how human beings can live in harmony despite their differences.

Of course there have been moments in history when racial tension has bubbled over into racially motivated violence. The Draft Riots led to the Mayor's Committee on Unity by Executive Order, which eventually became today's Commission on Human Rights. The Crown Heights Riots of August 1991 saw violence and general havoc as Jews and African Americans living in Crown Heights, Brooklyn, got a bit hot under the collar because of perceived discrimination issues.

Food & Drink

New York may be the city that never sleeps, but it's also the city that always eats - no matter what time of day or night it is, you can get yourself a little bit of what you fancy. A cream cheese bagel at 05:30? Chinese food at midnight? It's all possible.

The jumble of ethnicities in the city certainly results in varied cuisine - Italian, Mexican, American, Jewish and French are some of the more common ones, but that doesn't mean you can't find a huge range of Vietnamese, Indian, Greek, Japanese and African specialities as well. You'll be able to eat your way around the world (just make sure you wear your stretchy pants).

Because of the frenetic pace of the working week, New Yorkers don't usually get the chance to take a lingering lunch. Enter the convenience of that great New York institution - the deli. Ready-cooked meals and a range of sandwiches are all just a pair of tongs away - just pile whatever you want into a

Street market

plastic box, get it weighed at the till, and wolf it down. Other 'hurry up' lunch options include hot dogs from street vendors or a gigantic slice of pizza, available at countless pizza places throughout the city - just follow your nose to find one. After you've chosen your slice, fold it in half lengthways and eat it using one hand only - while walking, if you want to look like an experienced New Yorker that is!

Dinner is totally different, and usually involves no rushing around at all. The evening meal is usually as much about socialising as it is about sustenance. Whether you decide to dress up for a fancy dinner at one of the city's top restaurants, or dress down for a casual meal with friends at a cafe or deli, you'll find plenty of venues where you can simply hang out for ages.

Language

English is the official language in New York, though with the many dialects and heavy, heavy accents (good luck in Staten Island) it might not always seem it. The large Hispanic population has made Spanish the unofficial second language, and walking through any of the five boroughs, your ears will ring with so many different tongues it's like a linguistic fanfare to internationalism.

Though shop signs, restaurant awnings and the occasional menu may be written in a foreign transcript, English dominates the signposts. Chinatown is perhaps the only exception where some form of Chinese or Mandarin script accompanies the English.

Religion

Just as New York is the place where anyone is welcome, so is it the place where any religion is tolerated. At the start of its history, there was a predominant Roman Catholic population, thanks to the large number of Irish immigrants. Not long after, however, a large Jewish community started forming, and exists to this day. Today, no one denomination or religion takes precedence. Whatever you believe in, you are free to practise your religion and the city has an exhaustive list of churches, temples, mosques and synagogues.

Many of New York's churches and synagogues are worth visiting, but perhaps St Paul's Chapel deserves a special mention. It was one of the few buildings in the WTC area to suffer no structural damage after the 9/11 attacks, and became a refuge for those involved in the rescue efforts.

St Patrick's Cathedral

Index

Explorer Products

Residents' Guides

All you need
to know about
living, working
and enjoying life
in these exciting
destinations

Abu Dhabi

Amsterdam *

Bahrain

Barcelona *

Dubai

Dublin *

Geneva

Hong Kong

Kuwait

London

New York

New Zealand *

Oman

Paris *

Qatar

Shanghai *

Singapore

Sydney

* Covers not final. Titles available 4th quarter 2007.

Mini Guides

Perfect pocket-sized
visitors' guides

 Abu Dhabi
 Amsterdam
 Bahrain

 Barcelona
 Dubai
 Dublin
 Hong Kong

 London
 New York
 New Zealand
 Oman

* Covers not
  final. Titles
  available 4th
  quarter 2007.

 Paris
 Shanghai
 Singapore
 Sydney

Activity Guides

Drive, trek, dive and swim... life will never be boring again

 off-road Oman
 trekking Oman
 UAE underwater

Mini Maps

Fit the city in
your pocket

* Covers not final. Titles available 4th quarter 2007.

Maps

Wherever you are, never get lost again

Photography Books

Beautiful cities caught through the lens.

Lifestyle Products & Calendars

The perfect accessories for a buzzing lifestyle

Explorer Team

Publisher
Alistair MacKenzie

Editorial
Managing Editor Claire England
Lead Editors David Quinn, Jane Roberts, Matt Farquharson, Sean Kearns, Tim Binks, Tom Jordan
Deputy Editors Helen Spearman, Jake Marsico, Katie Drynan
Editorial Assistants Ingrid Cupido, Mimi Stankova

Design
Creative Director Pete Maloney
Art Director Ieyad Charaf
Senior Designers Alex Jeffries, Iain Young, Motaz Al Bunai
Layout Manager Jayde Fernandes
Designers Hashim Moideen, Rafi Pullat, Shefeeq Marakkatepurath, Sunita Lakhiani
Cartography Manager Zainudheen Madathil
Cartographer Noushad Madathil
Design Admin Manager Shyrell Tamayo
Production Coordinator Maricar Ong

IT
IT Administrator Ajay Krishnan R.
Software Engineer Roshni Ahuja

Photography
Photography Manager Pamela Grist
Photographer Victor Romero
Image Editor Henry Hilos

Sales and Marketing
Area Sales Manager Stephen Jones
Marketing Manager Kate Fox
Retail Sales Manager Ivan Rodrigues
Retail Sales Coordinator Kiran Melwani
Sales & Marketing Administrator Jamie Dino
Distribution Supervisor Matthew Samuel
Distribution Executives Ahmed Mainodin, Firos Khan, Mannie Lugtu
Warehouse Assistant Mohammed Kunjaymo
Drivers Mohammed Sameer, Shabsir Madathil

Finance and Administration
Administration Manager Andrea Fust
Accounts Assistant Cherry Enriquez
Administrator Enrico Maullon
Driver Rafi Jamal

Many thanks to Jennifer Keeney Sendrow, AnneLise Sorenson, Erin Donnelly, Amanda Scott, Dana Micheli, Rania Adwan, Karim Farid, Leonard Jacobs, Vadim Liberman.
Photographers: Pamela Grist, Jane Roberts, Louise Denly, Tilo Richter, Tom Jordan.